SHE MOVES THROUGH THE BOOM

For my father

She Moves
through the Boom

Ann Marie Hourihane

SITRIC BOOKS

First published 2000 by
SITRIC BOOKS LTD
62–63 Sitric Road, Arbour Hill,
Dublin 7, Ireland

A CIP record for this title is available from
The British Library.

1 3 5 7 9 10 8 6 4 2

ISBN 1 903305 03 9

*Some names of people interviewed for this book
have been changed.*

Set in Georgia
Printed in Ireland by ColourBooks, Baldoyle, Dublin

CONTENTS

1

[coffee]

The pub closest to our office, Maguire's, was renovated recently; but it had never really been old. Maguire's used to have a long bar that ran the depth of the building. It had leather chairs and studded leather benches against the wall. These benches fooled nobody; they were too high to have ever been old. The old Maguire's was mock old, with a library/gentlemen's club sort of feel. Knowledgable drinkers regarded it with suspicion. Our colleague Michael Hand used to say, 'Maguire's isn't a pub, it's a fucking hotel.'

Now Maguire's is sort of Eighties Barcelona chic. It has huge circular mirrors with deep wooden frames. These mirrors first appeared in Dublin in U2's Clarence hotel. They have been widely copied. I have one over my own mantelpiece at home, bought at cost, and much admired.

In the new Maguire's, huge plywood curves, which have no function, dip to where the dado rail used to be. The new chairs are upholstered in a light beige, and each table is dominated by one chair with a tall back, perhaps six feet high. Each tall beige chair is waiting for a blonde who's got her colour just right.

The serving area is now a crushed little thing, directly opposite the new door, with mirrors and glass shelving at the back of it. There is hardly room for the tiny Spanish waitress to stand with her tray. There's a cappuccino machine. Someone has built a cubicle against one wall of the pub, a modern snug with a three-sided counter where you can sip coffee on a stool.

After the renovation a little leaflet was left on each of the new circular tables. It was called *Coffee by Matthew Algie*, and it folded out to explain the options: 'Espresso, a small but potent coffee served black, in a small demitasse cup or glass. Characterised by a flavour and aroma so intense they bite. ... Macchiato, a small strong coffee with a delicate first impression, created by placing a small amount of foamed milk on top of the crema. Served in a small demitasse cup or glass ...' And so on, through Ristretto ('An extra-strong espresso, using the same amount of coffee, but half the quantity of water. A real pick-me-up, not to be confused with a double espresso'), Cappuccino, Caffé Latte and the rest. A small sepia diagram, with arrows, accompanies each explanation.

We go to Maguire's after the Tuesday editorial meeting at our newspaper. When the newsroom was being renovated, the editorial meetings were actually held in Maguire's. It's a good job poor Mixer Hand is dead, we said, the first time we met in the renovated Maguire's. We scanned the coffee leaflet for spelling mistakes and found none. Under the new regime you got a little biscuit with your coffee.

'I didn't get a biscuit,' said Nell McCafferty, who is a Northern republican. But she did, it was hiding out of sight behind her cup.

A smart woman in a grey trouser suit, with good make-up and carrying some fashionable shopping bags, came in and sat in the new-style snug. She lit a cigarette and drank cappuccino on one of the high stools. You dress up for town, you paint your liner onto swollen lids at seven-thirty in the bloody morning. Looking good for the traffic jams.

'They're attracting a better class of woman,' I said.

'Better than us?' said Nell.

'Better than us,' I said.

*

As you walk from the Yellow car park towards the Liffey Valley shopping centre you can make out the words '... Best Coffee'. You can't see the beginning of this slogan from the Yellow car park (Liffey Valley's car parks are colour-coded), where your car looks lonely on a Monday morning.

Liffey Valley shopping centre is long and low and beige in colour. It could be an airport, it could be a factory, it could be a hospital. One arm of it ends in Marks and Spencer, and the other in a fourteen-screen cinema. On a Thursday night in Liffey Valley the queue at the cash machine, fifteen people long, is made up mainly of very young couples who don't look married.

The coffee slogan is up on the second floor of the central tower, on what you soon discover is the South Beach Food Court. As you approach the shopping centre over empty tarmac the whole slogan appears before you. 'The World's Best Coffee', it says.

Liffey Valley is an experience; its promotional brochure says so.

The cover shows a young couple in ribbed knitwear embracing warmly. The slogan here is 'Liffey Valley, Where the M50 Meets the N4'. This would be admirably clear if only Dubliners knew the names of all the new roads. As it is, the only people who can confidently identify the N4, which goes to Sligo, are people from Sligo and property developers. Tom Gilmartin, the man who planned the Liffey Valley shopping centre, falls into both categories. Tom Gilmartin has never changed his accent, people say approvingly, even though he has lived in England for years. It's the little things that we take pleasure in.

The history of Liffey Valley should have been played out by men wearing straw hats and braces, sweating under ceiling fans and slapping flies, not men with grey hair and rimless glasses and anonymous suits like Liam Lawlor, Owen O'Callaghan and Frank Dunlop, beavering away under the grey skies of the M50, at a site called Quarryvale.

The man who co-owns the Liffey Valley shopping centre

now is Owen O'Callaghan, who built his first shopping centre in his home town of Ballincollig in County Cork. He went on to build more in Athlone, in Limerick, in Waterford, and in Cork city. In another country, all these shopping centres would not be important. In Ireland, shopping centres are national events, little patches of history, filling in the gaps in our development as we reach across the Atlantic, or the Irish Sea. A friend of mine remembers being brought to Dublin from County Cork on a school trip, to see the country's first suburban shopping centre, in Stillorgan. That was in 1966. We were mad with excitement about Stillorgan shopping centre then. It seemed to provide the only hope that one day we might live like the people we saw on television.

The facilities at Liffey Valley include 'shopmobility' (free hire of wheelchairs and scooters for the disabled, disabled parking, disabled toilets), the hire of children's buggies (deposit required), the hire of little tykes' bikes (deposit required), faxing and photcopying, job vacancy notices, First Aid, and Lost and Found. 'Just ask any of our staff for help!' it says on the back of the lavatory door. Anyone can come to Liffey Valley, as long as they have a car.

Oscar Wilde has already arrived. 'Oscar Wilde at Liffey Valley,' says the sign at Eason's newsagent and bookshop. Oscar is part of Eason's promotion of Irish writers, and there are pictures of the most famous ones hanging above the entrance to Eason's on the Gallery, which is on the way to the Western Rotunda.

The woman in Eason's is very pleased with the pictures. 'The one of Brendan Kennelly is fantastic,' she says.

You sit for a while on a bench facing Eason's and Champion Sports, with your back to the Ladies. From the bench you can look at the pictures of Ireland's dead authors hanging outside Eason's. 'In Ireland we have an imagination that is fiery, magnificent and tender.' J.M. Synge said that, apparently. Behold Beckett, Shaw, Wilde, Yeats and Synge: Irish Protestant males, a retailer's nightmare. Or look at the living authors: Maeve Binchy, Roddy Doyle, Nuala Ní Dhomhnaill, Seamus Heaney, Edna O'Brien, Brendan Kennelly. Catholic shoppers. Catholic advertisers, in Kennelly's case.

'The Future Is Champion' is the Champion Sports slogan. But they don't have any pool shoes in a size six. They have coloured Puma pool shoes in a sizes four to five, or seven to eight. And they have Speedo pool shoes in black only, in sizes three to four.

While the girl is in the stock room, looking for your shoes, a young male shop assistant is saying that he has not sold a pair of socks in Champion Sports since he started working there. A female shop assistant says that socks are where she gets all her multi-sales from. They laugh. But they definitely don't have any pool shoes in a size six.

You can't get coffee on the ground floor of Liffey Valley, unless you count a tiny container of *coffea arabica* which sells at £3.79 for 6cl, at the Boots homeopathic counter. *Coffea* is used, in tiny quantities, to treat symptoms like over-stimulation, stress, insomnia, having too many thoughts.

The woman on Boots' Clinique counter is talking about the South Beach Food Court. 'It's like a swimming pool,' she says. 'Have you ever been up there when the children are out of school? All you can hear is children shouting and that sort of empty sound.' She usually takes her breaks in Boots' staff canteen. She isn't sure if she's working on the Western Rotunda or on the Gallery. All she knows is that the Gallery is very long if you forget anything in Marks' and have to walk the whole way back during your lunch hour.

Boots is one of the three anchor stores, all British, at Liffey Valley. The other two are C & A and Marks and Spencer. Marks and Spencer is at the other end of the Gallery from Boots, on the Eastern Rotunda. You have to pass lots of branches of the smaller chains, like Top Shop and Envy, to get to it. In Portadown shopping centre, you now remember, there is a shop called Paranoia.

The girl who serves me in Marks and Spencer says she's sorry she ever came to work in Liffey Valley. You don't know what it's like, she says. She used to work at Marks and Spencer in Mary Street, off O'Connell Street. At least there was a bit of life in town. Together we look out into the bright Eastern Rotunda, where people are actually strolling. The girl is leaving in the summer to work on a boat in the Bahamas.

You glide up to the South Beach Food Court on an escalator. The first thing you see here is a small sign hanging from thin chains between two plastic palm trees. 'Welcome to South

Beach', says the sign. It tells you that South Beach Food Court was opened by Mr Bruce Singer, President of Miami Beach Chamber of Commerce. Underneath, in pots, sit two real parlour palms.

The South Beach Food Court is a re-creation of Miami, between the M50 and the N4. 'Someone in Grosvenor Holdings,' says Mr Singer on the phone from Miami Beach, 'I think his name was Steve, was a frequent visitor to South Florida and Miami Beach, and he came up with this concept for the Food Court. I spent a considerable amount of time with Steve coming up with information and photos for the concept. South Beach has really become a brand name which we are exporting.'

Mr Singer and a colleague were brought over from Miami Beach to Dublin for a week. The ribbon cutting was performed by Mr Singer and the Duke of Westminster, who owns Grosvernor Holdings, which has a 50 per cent stake in Liffey Valley; but only Mr Singer was commemorated on the plaque. 'A very collegial, friendly type of gentleman,' says Mr Singer of the Duke.

The re-creation of Miami in Liffey Valley is achieved mainly through signs. Like the one advertising 'Condos', with the phone number of the real estate company, Sunco, underneath. Little rays of sunlight come out of the 'o' in Sunco. There's a sign for the Miami City Ballet, and for a Hurricane Evacuation Bus Pick-Up Site. There is a mural, in the style of the old *New Yorker* cartoon, of a Miamian's View of the World. First of all there are the streets of Miami. Then there is Palm Beach. Then there is the sea, and across the sea, in the dim distance, are two green hills labelled Ireland and Scotland.

In front of the Miamian's View of the World people drink coffee from paper cups under a blue haze of cigarette smoke.

There is a slot machine on the wall which once dispensed Genuine Bayer Aspirin, the wonder drug that works wonders. Two packets of two tablets, 325mg of Genuine Bayer Aspirin, 50 cents.

The women who clean the South Beach Food Court wear blue and purple shirts and waistcoats, with 'South Beach Food Court' written on the back. They are in their forties and fifties. They clear and wipe tables, and empty ashtrays, talking to each other all the time.

The woman in Eason's had recommended the Kylemore Café for coffee. 'Their chairs are real relaxing,' she said. The South Beach Food Court also contains McDonald's; Spud-U-Like for baked potatoes; Harry Ramsden's for fish and chips; KFC for chicken; the Wok Station for Oriental food (it offers boneless ribs); La Croissanterie; and BB's Coffee and Muffins.

I choose BB's Coffee and Muffins because it is home to the slogan 'The World's Best Coffee'. BB's offers Cappuccino, Mugaccino, Skinniccino, Espresso, Long Black, Flat White, Latte, Latte Macchiator, Mocha, Dutch Coffee, Vienna Coffee. You can also get BB's Tea, Earl Grey or English Breakfast Tea. Or Herbal or Fruit Teas. Or Hot Chocolate. Or Chocomallow. Or Hot Soup, which today is potato and leek, and scorched brown. With the soup I have roasted vegetables. I also have a Skinniccino, which is made with skimmed milk. It is a mistake.

Coffee breaks are a real problem in the Liffey Valley, says Caroline, who works in Oasis, particularly if you smoke. Each shop has its own little canteen out the back, but you're not allowed to smoke there, or anywhere in the shopping centre besides the South Beach Food Court. The girls end up standing in one of the car parks, smoking.

At the end of the week, with cash running low, you can't go for lunch up in the Kylemore, which is the shop assistants' favourite restaurant in the Liffey Valley. And you can't afford to be buying your sandwiches in Marks and Spencer every day, either.

'You'd miss a little Tesco or something,' says Caroline. 'But it's a nice place to work. All the staff are very friendly. It's a nice centre. We're getting there, we're getting there.'

*

The only place at Liffey Valley that is still called Quarryvale is the local-authority estate that lies alongside it. The only shops in Quarryvale are the Green Garden Chinese take-away, a mini-market, and Mick's, which sells newspapers and milk and bread and comics and nappies, cashes social security cheques, and provides a pay phone; the two phone booths outside the shops lasted twenty-four hours. Mick's actually has sawdust on the floor, if it has been raining. Every morning at eight o'clock when he opens his shop, Mick picks up about twenty pence worth of change from the ground outside. He has started to notice that even small children disdain change now. Sometimes they won't take ten pence back off him.

One of the striking things about Mick's is that, for a modern shop, it seems underlit. The other striking thing about Mick's is that it is sandwiched among eleven derelict units in a one-storey, graffitti-laden bomb site that serves about 3,000 people. When you see the shops on the Quarryvale estate you can hear yourself gasp out loud. Last September the plan to revitalize this block was already two years behind schedule. Even the new scheme doesn't contain any plans for privately run shops; this Quarryvale isn't anyone's idea of a retail opportunity.

Mick also leases the mini-market beside the newsagents, which has an Asian feel, perhaps because it is spotlessly clean and strangely narrow. It sells two types of Maxwell House coffee, granules and powder, and both are £2.39.

The other eight shop units here are unoccupied. The Spar and the hairdresser's closed down a long time ago. So did the butcher's, the bookie's, and the chemist's.

Liffey Valley was a disaster for the Quarryvale housing estate. No one in Quarryvale shops at Liffey Valley, because they can't afford it. They shop where they used to shop before it was built: at Dunne's Stores at the Mill in Clondalkin, at Crazy Prices in Ballyfermot, or in town.

You need a taxi if you want to go into town. 'They moved the bus stop. I've a family of nine, that's a lot of bags, you couldn't carry them all on the bus,' says Margaret Waldron, who has her little granddaughter with her in a buggy. Taxis, says Christine Moore, make a fortune out of Quarryvale. At a bus stop you wouldn't know where you are. Women getting a bus at seven o'clock in the morning to go into work in town 'were met by men who had been out sleeping rough all night', says Margaret Waldron. 'Were met by men exposing themselves,' says Christine, who used the buses to get into work in St Patrick's mental hospital in the city. 'I said "Feck this" and took driving lessons.'

Christine's son is twenty and he's never been in town. Christine is glad of this because she considers the city centre to be terribly dangerous. 'You'd be killed in town over a taxi, that's the way it's gone.' Some young people in Quarryvale, say Margaret and Christine, fearing the muggings that can take place round the shopping centre at night, will get a taxi to Liffey Valley if they are going to the cinema there, even though the complex is clearly visible from their houses. 'The youth go there,' says Margaret. The youth.

*

On a brief drive round Quarryvale you see two burned-out cars, one blocking a walkway, and windscreen glass everywhere. 'They steal the cars or buy them off the Travellers,' says Angela Boylan. Her car is a lovely Opel Corsa. She got the financing down in Clondalkin, after the people in the local

Renault building at the Liffey Valley development wouldn't return her calls. 'I'm not joking you, I must have rang them fifty times.'

Angela's is a two-income family. She works in the City West hotel – her daughter Kim works there too during the summer – and her husband Paddy is a console operator at Texaco. He works nights. He needs a car. She needs a car. I drop ash on the upholstery of the Corsa. 'Don't mind, it needs a hoovering anyway,' says Angela. Angela and Paddy's house is hung with paintings of horses and of John Wayne. 'This place is little Beiruit,' says Paddy.

Angela, who used to be a member of the residents' association, is providing a rough guide to drug dealers' houses on the Quarryvale estate, but I lose track. Somehow it all comes back to shops. 'I always say that after eight o'clock at night it's easier for our kids to get a £10 deal than it is for them to get a 10p ice pop,' says Angela.

Traffic lights are only now going up outside Saint Bernadette's primary school and Saint Kevin's senior school, where a child was knocked down and killed two years ago. Saint Bernadette's is on the Coldcut Road. On the bank between Coldcut Road and Greenfort Close you can see marks from where five cars were recently burned.

You go round by the Old Tower Castle estate, a small maze of red-brick bungalows and broken glass, and see the old tower, which is very small, held hostage by fencing and surrounded by new houses. Angela's road is Shancastle Drive,

Margaret's road is Shancastle Avenue, Christine's road is Shancastle Lawns.

The Liffey Valley shopping centre divided the Quarryvale estate. People in the houses nearest the shopping centre were paid £3,000 per house in compensation for, amongst other things, having an entrance to the estate blocked off. The people at the other end got nothing – 'even though people drive through here at fifty mile an hour', says Christine Moore, who has the caution of someone who learned to drive late. 'That's at the weekend, when they make their fortune over there.'

According to Angela, the Clondalkin Addiction Support Programme had been evicted from the community centre by the residents' association – 'and they were the anchor tenant'. So the community centre has become run-down 'and too expensive'. The new, extended community centre will be a white elephant, she says.

Angela joined the Socialist Party, of which local TD Joe Higgins is the only parliamentary representative, as a consequence of her experience in community politics. 'Joe Higgins is the only TD who tells the truth.'

Angela and Paddy have three daughters and three horses. But when the local authorities moved against horses on working-class estates three years ago, they had to move the animals from a field off the nearby Fonthill Road, which was partly owned by Liam Lawlor, TD.

'Liam Lawlor sat here in my living room,' says Angela, waving her arm towards Kim, 'talking about the horses.' Now the horses are kept in Kinnegad and Athgoe. Angela's youngest daughter, Audrey, is borderline autistic. 'I had them in Irish dancing, I had them in the majorettes, I had them in karate, but nothing would do them only the horses.'

Horses are the only thing that Audrey shows emotion about. 'That and pushing babies around,' says Angela.

*

In the garden of 46 Dromheath Avenue, in Lady's Well, Mulhuddart, just left at the church of St Luke's the Evangelist, which looks like a Protestant church in America, a fine brown pony stands grazing. I know very little about ponies but even I can see that this one has a touch of class about him. He is surrounded by three or four boys in their early teens who watch him from the wall as though they were his mother. Ponies are to some teenage boys what babies are to some teenage girls.

Mulhuddart used to be a world away from Quarryvale and the Liffey Valley shopping centre and Clondalkin and Neilstown and everywhere on the south side of the river. Mulhuddart is on the north side of the Liffey, on the old road to Navan. But now Mulhuddart, which is near Blanchardstown, is part of the mess that has thrust through west County Dublin. You can get to Liffey Valley shopping centre from Blanchardstown in less than twenty minutes on the M50, an arc of motorway which sweeps through fields and industrial buildings and, dimly visible from the dual carriageway, hundreds and hundreds and hundreds of houses. The M50 is home to what must the longest hedge in the world; I think it is hawthorn, but I can't stop to check. History finishes here. Now we are going to live like everybody else.

As you enter the toll booth on the West-Link Bridge, scrabbling for change, you do not know that your car is one of the 69,000 to 70,000 cars that pass through it every day. That added up to 23.3 million vehicles in 1999. That added up to an £11.65 millon profit for National Toll Roads at the end of 1999. As you leave the toll booth you see a sign which says 'Prepare To Merge'.

This is what the M50 is for. Mulhuddart, Clonee and Blanchardstown in the north and Clondalkin, Neilstown and Tallaght in the south have merged into an alternative city, an alternative country. Perhaps it is the way that you look *down* on this landscape from the M50 that makes you feel you are somewhere else. Flat, sprawling, confused and centreless, west Dublin is now New Jersey. Somewhere out there is its Frank Sinatra, its Bruce Springsteen.

It is all a consequence of the patchwork planning that started with the Myles Wright Plan in 1967. Myles Wright was the Liverpool University professor of town planning at a time when British town planning was creating places like modern Birmingham, and moving the working classes out to suburbia. (Myles Wright, now in his nineties, lives in Cheshire.) It was said that Labour governments did more to destroy Britain's cities after the war than the Luftwaffe had done during it.

Wright's plan proposed four new towns in west Dublin: Tallaght, Lucan, Clondalkin, and Blanchardstown. They exploded in a flurry of social housing, like the Quarryvale estate and Mulhuddart, and private housing, like Laurel Lodge in Castleknock, which was developed by Patrick Gallagher, who was Charles Haughey's friend and donor. In the late Seventies and Eighties there were protests from the people who had bought on private estates, and from those who were renting on public estates, about the poor quality of the buildings.

West Dublin, one of the fastest-growing urban areas in Europe, is a planning disaster. It smells like teen spirit but is seriously short of football pitches. Yet you don't have to be in Blanchardstown shopping centre for very long to know that this is the real future, which has grown up unloved and unobserved.

In May 1991, when the Lucan–Clondalkin town centre was re-located to Quarryvale, Green Properties, which owned the site for Blanchardstown shopping centre, responded by threatening to abort their plans, because they could not imagine that two huge retail developments could thrive so close together.

The threatened cancellation of the planned Blanchardstown shopping centre became a huge issue in the local elections a month later. People in Mulhuddart went on protest marches to support the proposed Blanchardstown shopping centre, which was to be built by a private company and run as a business to make money out of them. Twelve re-zoning councillors, including Liam Lawlor, lost their seats in that election. Blanchardstown shopping centre got back on track and, crucially,

Dunne's Stores, the flagship of affordable shopping for the working class, agreed to come in as an anchor tenant.

'I won't shop in Dunne's Stores,' says Patricia, who lives in Palmerstown Woods, near Lucan, and doesn't want her real name in a book. 'I just don't like all the things that happened over the years.'

Years ago my mother wouldn't shop in Dunne's Stores because she didn't like the way they treated their female workers. 'Women my age, having to ask some young pup in a suit to approve a cheque,' she said. Shopping is an emotional business. But Patricia, who shops in Tesco in Ballyfermot or in the Square in Tallaght, is unusual in her boycott of Dunne's Stores. The rest of us turn up at Dunne's every week with our money, just as blithely as Ben Dunne once turned up at the front door of Charles Haughey, with the bank drafts in his pocket. Convenience is the thing now.

You can see the blue banners of Blanchardstown shopping centre from the M50. 'We were lost without it,' says Natalie, who is visiting her sister in Lady's Well in Mulhuddart. She is heavily pregnant with her second child. Natalie wouldn't go to Liffey Valley. She couldn't afford it and anyway 'there's too many English shops up there'.

'The new centre is just fantastic, it's not even too far to walk there. You can get the 238 minibus right there and the 220 pases right through it. It has everything.' Natalie is renting with her partner in Clondalkin but can't wait to get a house back in the Lady's Well estate, where the houses are built in blocks of four, and grouped in cul de sacs off Dromheath Avenue. Natalie doesn't know about the Dromheath bit: 'It's just the Avenue.' Like many people in the Blanchardstown area, Natalie refers to the shopping centre as 'the town centre'. Blanchardstown shopping centre isn't just the only game in town, it has become the town itself.

Before the Blanchardstown shopping centre was built, says Joe Higgins, TD, you couldn't buy a pair of socks in Mulhuddart. The interesting thing is that you still can't. Mulhuddart village has Gleeson's pub, Guilio's Takeaway, Tara Video, the Bike Shop, the Barber Shop, J. P. AutoCare Car Valeting and the Village Take Out. The road that has brought you here, northwards from Blanchardstown shopping centre, is rural with old trees on either side and the gates of an old house discreetly hiding a Traveller encampment. Now the traffic on this road is intense, leading as it does to Damastown Industrial Estate which houses the huge IBM and Yamanouchi factories.

The Mulhuddart Self Service shop has a sign up asking its customers to pay for their petrol in advance. 'There have been so many drive-offs,' says the sign, apologetically. 'You want to be a tough woman to work here,' says Joan, who doesn't look tough at all, but tanned and bare-armed in a knitted top. She is selling very small sweets to very small boys. 'Give us twenty Lipsticks,' says a very small boy. 'Thank you.'

Basil McKeon, who leases the shop and forecourt from Shell Ireland, has the greatest difficulty holding on to staff like Joan. As soon as you get any good staff they are poached, he says. There is a slight, bald security man on the door, who looks nervous. It used to take Basil five minutes to drive into Blanchardstown village to go to the bank or the post office. Now it can take up to half an hour.

Mulhuddart Self Service is open from seven in the morning until eleven o'clock at night, Monday to Saturday, and from eight in the morning until ten at night on Sunday. Apart from petrol it sells cigarettes, groceries and confectionery. The shop has been open for thirteen years. 'So many changes in that time,' says Basil. 'It's been constant road works. First of all the bypass ten years ago, then the shopping centre. Now they're shutting the Cruiserath Road. I don't think they knew what they were doing with the roads here. I don't think it was properly planned.'

'It's a very mixed area,' says Joan. 'But you can see the difference the shopping centre has made. You see it in the cars. The cars round here used to be dreadful. You see it in the women. Women are working. They're going on holidays.'

Excuse me, says a woman behind me. Can I pay for £10 worth of petrol, if you don't mind? She has a 00 reg car and a brown suit. It's terrible to be ignored in shops. It's infuriating when the assistant won't meet your eye, when they are talking to someone else, and conduct your entire transaction – scanning your purchase, taking your money, ringing it up, giving you your change – without saying a word to you at all. You don't need this at the end of a long day, when you are paying for your bloody petrol in advance.

In Blanchardstown shopping centre there seems to be some sort of arrangement that shops of the same type are placed opposite each other. So McDonald's is opposite Burger King and both are pretty full. Boots is opposite Vision Express. EBS building society is opposite the ACC bank and both have small queues. Near the ACC is Variety World, where you can buy a large Laurel and Hardy lamp for £79.99, or a crystal banjo for £14.99. The best thing in Variety World is Big Mouth Billy Bass, a mounted fish who sings 'Take Me to the River' and 'Don't Worry, Be Happy'. You just stand in front of Billy and laugh. The Queen has one. 'They were all over Blackpool,' says a woman with an English accent to her friend. In McCabe's Pharmacy the woman on the Clarins counter is saying, 'I think the Age Control is better myself.' In Tommy's Wonderland there is a shelf marked 'Mary Help of Christians'. Tommy's sells school uniforms. It also sells an artificial swallow's nest, full of swallow chicks who are reaching towards their ministering parent. The swallows and their parent are a plaque for the side of your house. The plaque costs £1.99.

Over by the Pokemon section in Tommy's, just inside the door, is a huge transparent case of yellow Winnie-the-Poohs. A boy of about thirteen and a much smaller boy put money in the slot and the older boy starts to move the metal claw, to pick up one of the bears. 'I'm going for that one,' he says. But something happens – I miss it – and the boy drops the bear from the claw and suddenly his turn is over and he is twenty feet away from the machine, ashamed. The younger boy is unfazed, and takes the controls. 'How much was your go?' he calls after the bigger boy's turned back. 'How much was your go?' But the older boy does not reply. He is vanishing down an aisle.

Blanchardstown shopping centre is full of teenagers, and everyone else, and it isn't even the weekend. You can smoke on the walkways. Coffee is sold from a little stall called Friends. There are children everywhere. If Liffey Valley is Stansted Airport then Blanchardstown is Heathrow in peak season. P. Gleeson Family Butcher is packed. It is advertising Five Fresh Chicken Fillets for £3.99, Three Gigot Pork Chops for 99p and Low Salt Collar Bacon, Any Weight Cut!

Upstairs the curved-glass roof is supported by white ribs, like a Victorian railway station or the inside of a whale. The information desk is backed by a bank of thirty-two television screens, on which a young black couple, partly clothed, are embracing. A plaque beside the information desk says that Blanchardstown shopping centre was opened by the then Taoiseach, John Bruton, and his wife Finola, in 1994.

The entire shop frontage of Blanchardstown shopping centre is said to be equivalent to that of Grafton Street, but there are probably more shops for teenagers here. Top Shop is selling covers for mobile phones at £14.99. They come in pastel colours – one is a tri-colour with a shamrock in the middle – and 'Clubbing Cutie' is written on each of them. You can get one inscribed with the slogan 'Rich Bitch' or 'On The Pull'. One white phone cover has mock road signs on it, and the little road signs say 'No Limp Dicks' or 'Wrong Time of the Month'.

A steep-incline sign says '60% Minimum Erection Before Entry.' It's hard to explain.

Aoife O'Reilly, Anna Smith and Sinéad McDonald are all sixteen and have very clean hair. They're from Lambourne in Clonsilla, and never go into town. The bus drops them right outside the door. They're standing now at a slim pillar outside the cinema. 'It's deadly. It has everything. It's a good place. Everyone goes to the cinema every time they come here. It's a tradition.'

Aoife, Anna and Sinéad don't really go to Liffey Valley. 'It has very few shops. It's well out of the way.'

Blanchardstown shopping centre is open all weekend – that's its busiest time – and the Leisure Centre, opposite the main centre but part of it, is open twenty-four hours a day. Inside the Leisure Centre it is night-time in America. There is an eighteen-lane bowling alley, countless pool tables, the Q-Zar laser game, dodgem cars, professional wrestling flickering on all the televisions, unidentifiable music, and ranks and ranks of games machines. Two little boys puck a disc back and forth on the table between them. 'Ice hockey,' they say shortly.

Keith Maher is very tall and fourteen, and laughs in a kind of teenage agony as he talks. His friend Mark is much smaller, and suspicious, even though he is fifteen. They are from Corduff. They come here most days, spending what they earn as lounge boys in the Brookwood on the football machines – 'Though we can't work much because we're under age.' All their money is spent in the Centre, in the cinema, on clothes in

Champion Sports or in the Leisure Centre. It's seventy-five pence to get in. 'That's a bit of a rip-off,' says Mark. 'You shouldn't have to pay to get in. It's a pound a shot and you have to play a good few times before you get good at it.'

Keith and Mark aren't allowed in to the Leisure Centre after eleven o'clock at night, when it becomes over-eighteens. That's when you get the after-pub crowd and, later, the taxi drivers coming in for their breakfasts. The Fact File says that Blanchardstown shopping centre is visited by 280,000 shoppers each week. The Fact File says that 650,000 people live within twenty minutes' drive of Blanchardstown shopping centre, but in fact they all seem to be here, all the time. They are hopping on buses, towing trolleys – 'Trolley Management', says the little jeep – and crossing the road to Petstop Superstore and McGuirks Golf, and to the Leisure Centre where you can drink a cup of Nescafé in the diner and think, 'Where do we live? Where do we live?'

*

Lyons' butcher shop in Ranelagh village is closing down, and of course you are sympathetic. The butchering trade has been devastated by the supermarkets, parking restrictions, and vegetarianism. Lyons', a neat and tidy shop (Mr Lyons' favourite part of his work is presentation), seems to be patronized exclusively by female pedestrians in search of two lamb chops. Mr Lyons is a dapper man who wears a red and white striped apron. I have already spoken to him about the possibility of buying his old butcher's chopping block for our kitchen.

At Mr Lyons' large modern bungalow, which is situated just behind the shop and has ample parking space for Mr Lyons' BMW, Mr Lyons says he's selling not because of the supermarkets – business is good – but because he is tired. He can't get staff. Young people don't want to go into butchering, to work weekends. On the other hand, he thinks butchering will revive. 'If I was a younger man I'd buy in an area like this and in three years you'd clean up.'

Mr Lyons is having lamb chops for his dinner tonight. He lives alone: 'I have enough of people all day.' He is separated from his wife, who lives nearby in Mount Anville with their three children. Mr Lyons protects me from his small, aggressive dog, who looks very fit.

When he first came to Ranelagh, twenty-five years ago, there were ten butcher shops in this prosperous suburban village. He bought from a man called Patrick Walsh, who was from Malahide and had the premises as a pork shop. Patrick Walsh was killed in a car accident two weeks after he retired, Mr Lyons says. Now, as commuters roll past the shop each day, one to a car, there are two butcher shops in Ranelagh. Even O'Gorman's, the famous sausage-maker, has closed down. O'Gorman's is now a café, selling cappuccino, caffé latte and espresso, as well as vegetable wraps.

At one stage Mr Lyons employed two butchers, an apprentice, a sausage maker, and a van man. Now it is just him. He doesn't want to work fourteen-hour days anymore. 'My sister died young, at forty-six. She was President of Galway Bay Golf Club and she was always asking me to go down and play golf with her. I was always saying, "Maybe next year, maybe next year." I never went. When my sister was going she told me that I'd have to slow down. That affected me.'

In Mr Lyons' opinion it was the government policy of decentralization that broke Ranelagh, by moving young civil servants out of the city. When he bought his premises twenty-five years ago there were eight people renting the three-bed-room apartment above the shop. Now there are four. As Ranelagh became re-gentrified, houses that had once contained ten people reverted to being occupied by a single family.

'I could have bought a house in Mountainview Road for £35,000 only twenty years ago,' says Mr Lyons regretfully. 'I could have bought a house on Sandford Road for £40,000.' The question that is everywhere in Dublin – What the hell were we doing twenty years ago, out at the cinema, drinking in pubs, waiting for buses, when we should have been borrowing every penny we could and buying property? – hovers in Mr Lyons' kitchen, between us as we talk.

Mr Lyons built this bungalow, the family house in Mount Anville, and a holiday home in Wexford, himself. The *Readers' Digest Complete Guide to DIY* is at his side as he speaks. 'I know what I'm doing,' he says. Today he got a phone call from the people who are building a house for him in his hometown of Mullingar to say that a JCB had a hit a sewer. That would panic a novice. Mr Lyons told them just to put a sleeve on the top of it and cover it in concrete.

For years Mr Lyons was thinking he would get out of butchering and buy a pub. But, workwise, that would have been out of the frying pan and into the fire. So he is going to rest for a little while and then move into developing, the buying and selling of property. The house in Mullingar will have seven bedrooms, 'all *en suite*'. He is hoping to provide B&B for the people who come to Mullingar to ride. There will be parking room for their horse boxes. Mr Lyons might think of putting some motorboats on to the lake for them.

Mr Lyons is fifty-five years old. His mother is eighty-five and still sows her own potatoes. 'I anticipate being quite busy,' says Mr Lyons. 'I call myself an entrepreneur. If I'd make money I'd go anywhere.'

As I'm leaving I ask again about the chopping block – that little flicker of greed, that dread of missing a bargain – from the shop, but Mr Lyons tells me that it is already sold.

*

I bought a cappuccino machine once, and two tins of Illy coffee pods, back in the days when cappuccino was a real treat. The whole lot cost me £164, more than I had ever spent on a Christmas present before. My mother is one of those people who always know what they want for Christmas.

My mother loves new things. She believes in technology and in progress. When we were teenagers, and drank Maxwell House, she came home with a tiny padlock for the phone. You can imagine the shock. We hadn't known that such a thing existed. But my mother found one, and was very pleased with it. She never lost the tiny keys for the padlock. She is a highly organized woman and she had too many teenagers to be sentimental about their telephone requirements.

In 1994 she had given up smoking and taken up drinking cappuccino instead. It was the latest thing. She searched out coffee shops that served cappuccino – and not many did back then. She rewarded herself after doing the grocery shopping by having a cup of cappuccino in the shopping centre. Cappuccino was her new thing.

The problem was that no one could work the cappuccino machine. After Christmas I phoned the shop where I had bought it, Cooke's Food Hall, which was part of the Cooke's Café empire that seemed to be marching down a little street in Dublin called Castle Market. Johnny Cooke told me to phone the distributor in Dundalk. The distributor in Dundalk said that we should bring the machine up to him, but we never did. When is anyone just passing Dundalk, so that they can drop in with a cappuccino machine?

We waited for New Year when my brother, the sole inheritor of my mother's technological skills, came home from London, so that he could fix it. He couldn't fix it. The cappuccino machine sat on my mother's kitchen window sill. It sat there for years. My mother would look at it and say, 'It's a shame. Even our Johnnie can't work it.'

Three years later I met a man who loved coffee and was good with his hands. He fixed the s-bend under my sink, and hung the big circular mirror over the fireplace, using a power drill. 'Great to have someone who's good at DIY,' said my mother. 'I have to do everything myself.'

She gave the cappuccino machine to him. He can't work it either. For three years it sat on the window sill of my back room, beside the clothes dryer. It was too expensive to throw away.

*

To get to Dundalk you take the Belfast train from what used to be Dublin's most dismal station, Connolly Station in Amiens Street. 'Choose your own favourite coffee,' says a sign. 'Irish,' you think, blackly. It is ten-thirty in the morning. You are probably an alcoholic.

Nothing can relieve the unloveliness of a Dublin crowd as we queue for our tickets amongst the cigarette butts, the unswept floor and the plywood hoardings. Amiens Street is being renovated. They apologize for our inconvenience. An African man tries to dislodge a rusting luggage trolley from a long line of rusting luggage trolleys. From one third-world country to another.

Dundalk was once a railway town. In 1949 its carriage shop

alone could field a full soccer team. Dundalk made boilers for the trains all over Ireland. There used to be a Dundalk saying: 'As deaf as a boiler-maker.'

In the Café Metz on Francis Street, Richard Martin, coffee importer, is explaining how the boilers on the Astoria cappuccino machines have to be enlarged for the Irish market, so that they can be used to make long espressos, or tea.

Café Metz has an Astoria espresso machine. Café Metz has a high bar counter facing the door, glass shelving against a mirror background, a copper pillar, wrought-iron chairs, a huge curved couch with velvet finish, basket lampshades, Spanish tiles, Spanish omelettes, thirty-seven staff. The wrought iron came from Armagh, the lighting came from Kilkenny.

Café Metz just sounded like a good name. It was only when some Europeans came in that the proprietors learned that Metz was a town in France that had had the hell bombed out of it during the Second World War. Café Metz is owned by the two Keogh brothers, who also own Mr Ridley's nightclub up on Park Street. With the Metz the Keoghs were aiming at people their own age – the thirties. People who were willing to try something new. The Metz serves homemade scones but it also serves scrambled eggs with smoked salmon and fresh figs, which must have taken some getting used to.

Martin Sheen came in one time when he was over filming in Cavan. He had the apple pie.

It is lunchtime. I am eating braised shank of lamb in the

Café Metz with Richard Martin. When Richard Martin was a boy, Jocelyn Street at lunchtime was a river of bicycles, eight or ten abreast, as the workers from the Great Northern Railway Locomotive Works and the shoe factories and Carroll's cigarette factory went home for their dinners. (Dundalk is the town that gave the world Sweet Afton cigarettes.) Richard's family imported cork, which was used for bottling in the local pubs. One time, in 1948, he and his father put an old Austin 10 on one of the cargo ships and sailed to Portugal, where they drove around the green north of that country. Now he imports coffee from Italy.

Richard used to be an altar boy with the man who fathered the Corrs, Gerry Corr. They were altar boys at the Redemptorist church in the town, too busy arguing over who was going to ring the bell to listen to the sermons, which were fiery. The Redemptorists were the storm-troopers of the Catholic Church. Dundalk was a rare home base for them. They toured the country on what were called missions. It was a Redemptorist mission to Limerick in the early years of the century which led to the pogrom against Limerick's Jews. Dundalk has a history of extremists.

Gerry Corr's father had a grocery shop round the corner from the Redemptorist church, where the Viva mini-mart now stands. Richard has no explanation for how the Corrs got to be so beautiful, though when pressed he remembers their late mother, Jean, being a smasher in her day. And Gerry, he supposes, must have been handsome. Irishmen of Richard's and my father's generation somehow regard male beauty, particularly their own, as a weakness. To notice another man's beauty would be rude.

Gerry Corr went to work in the ESB, and moonlighted playing at weddings with Jean. Their children hit the genetic jackpot, looks-wise. Jim Corr now wears clothes by John Rocha, Prada, Dolce & Gabbana, Comme des Garçons. He's bought a house in Dundalk and is having it painted in organic paint, which is produced locally by a young Swedish girl. She also decorated Richard's sister-in-law's beauty salon.

For the 1999 tour, Andrea's purple backless top and long grape skirt were designed by Marc O'Neill. The sweet thing about the Corr girls is that they look like Oasis girls, even though they wear John Rocha, Versace, and sometimes Chloe and Elspeth Gibson. Even their stylist admits they are not above buying in chain stores. They are a stylist's dream; just acres of cheekbone, hip bone and blue eye. They hardly have a stomach between them.

Richard Martin started importing coffee in 1990, when his other food importing business abruptly ended. At that time the Illy coffee company had 25 salesmen in Ireland who shifted 300 kilos of coffee per year. Richard's family of four girls and a boy were reared and he was able to give the new business his full attention. Now he's shifting 20 tonnes of coffee in Ireland each year.

He started by going to the Eurotoque restaurants. He brought his own tiny espresso machine and a weighing scales with him, in a bag. After each meeting he'd make the coffee. 'I really believed in the coffee,' he says.

Irish people's experience of coffee had been a bitter one, Richard found. Not only had the early cappuccino machines broken down, staff were not trained to use them. The grinders were set to take too much coffee (this was where his weighing scales came in). Worse still, the whole country was raddled by coffee made with the cheap Robusta bean, which grows at sea level and crops vigorously. Coffee made from the Robusta bean leaves a bitter taste on the back of the tongue, which, Richard says, isn't washed by saliva. The Robusta is half the price of ordinary coffee beans, and very high in caffeine.

'Commercially the Robusta was a disaster because no one ever had a second cup,' says Richard. 'They were too hyper on caffeine.' There you have the Eighties in a nutshell.

On the way back to Dublin from Dundalk (on the Enterprise train, thank God), the man across the aisle, a Northerner, is talking on his mobile phone. A big, handsome young man in jeans. He is speaking about some associate with whom he was severing a connection. 'You just get sick of earning four or five hundred pounds a time,' he said.

*

Le Coq Hardi is a very expensive restaurant, and it's not even new. It's been serving shellfish in rich sauces to businessmen for more than twenty years. If you go to Le Coq Hardi for dinner during the week there is a good chance you'll be the only woman there. Everyone else has a grey suit and a professional way with their knives.

For this reason Le Coq Hardi is not a great place for a romantic dinner for two. It's like having a double bed in a dormitory; you feel a bit exposed.

However, Le Coq Hardi is a great way of showing a woman that you, or your company, or somebody else's company, has lots and lots of money. It's the kind of place that men take women before they sleep with them, but never afterwards. It has an atmosphere of dulled sin.

It also has a private dining-room, and it is here that Charlie Haughey and his mistress, Terry Keane, were said regularly to dine. One estimate put Charlie's spending on Terry at two grand a month, and a lot of that was said to have gone on restaurants. All that cream. Charlie and Terry were the boom couple before the boom had even started.

I thought Le Coq Hardi's private dining room would be as sexy as all get out. Instead I found it to be a high and echoing dark green room, slightly musty, with a large table down one end. It was gloomy. Le Coq Hardi has an espresso machine made by Sacco, which the management is very happy with. It serves Mescela coffee, which is Italian. It also serves Kenco filter coffee.

*

In the Eighties I thought the Nicaraguan coffee campaign was a bunch of hippies in bright woolly sweaters, but it changed Eileen Banks's life. In 1986 she had already worked for two of the most successful state organizations in Ireland: the IDA, which scouted for foreign companies to invest in Ireland, and Bord Fáilte, which just scouted for foreigners. She also worked as volunteer for Women's Aid.

Politics was still personal then. The 1983 Pro-Life Amendment was really the death of the Irish Left, but for a while we didn't know, so we just kept walking. I say we, but I was not even a socialist. You didn't have to be a socialist to be a member of the Irish Left; you just had to want contraception. Through this modest commitment you'd end up knowing the entire membership of a Maoist group called Revolutionary Struggle. In Ireland you don't have to believe in God to define yourself as a Catholic. It's not what you believe in, it's what you're against. It's not what you're like, it's what the others are like. This is still the basis of Irish politics.

Ireland is too small for an alternative culture. In Britain, left-wing people wouldn't have a *Sun* reader as their friend. They left the families and the areas they had been born into. It was possible to live and work and sleep around without ever meeting a Tory; in fact, many left-wingers lived their lives to that specific end. They used to laugh amongst themselves about the misguided non-socialists they had met in the course of their non-busy days; no one was busy then. In Ireland that sort of sectarianism wasn't an option. We didn't have an Islington to run to.

In Ireland all politics is local. It is hard to maintain an undying hatred for the pro-lifers when Mrs Brady from round the corner, a lovely woman who was the mother of your brother's best friend in primary school, and baked birthday cakes for the entire neighbourhood, is outside the polling station with 'Vote Yes' leaflets in her hand. It is more than hard, it is embarrassing for you both.

In Britain, feminists were having to say that Mrs Thatcher wasn't really a woman. In Ireland, British sociologists stumbled around in a system that didn't conform to any of their rules at all. In the end the Irish Left melted into the professions, or journalism, or the civil service, or RTÉ, or, like Eileen Banks, into the IDA. But Eileen Banks kept going.

'The IDA was hugely succesful,' she says. 'It had a strong work ethic, and great company loyalty. I think they thought I was a leftie radical, but that was always viewed as something creative.'

Before Eileen took her career break she went to hear Daniel Ortega give a public lecture in Trinity College. 'I was absolutely fired by this. As an Irish person I could identify completely with a small country.'

Eileen was on the first work brigade that went out from Ireland to pick coffee in Nicaragua in January 1988. The brigade was bussed out from Nicaragua to an UPE, or state collective farm, which had once been the property of one of the big landowning families, near a town called Matagalpa.

They had arrived in January, in time for the coffee harvest.

Coffee was a vital cash crop to Nicaragua, and therefore to the Sandinista government.

The brigade walked out to the coffee fields at dawn, with the local people, and worked until five in the afternoon. They were in bed each night at eight.

Eileen doesn't know what sort of coffee she picked. 'The best coffee was exported,' she remembers. 'The coffee we drank was awful.'

On her return to Ireland Eileen went back to the IDA, and later worked with Forbairt, encouraging local businesses in the poorest parts of Ireland. Her Nicaraguan experience helped her when she visited small communities, she thinks. 'In Leitrim and Mayo there was no point in people waiting for the government to do something for you, you've got to do it yourself. And there's a much stronger level of awareness about development around the country now than there was in the Eighties. People look at the disparity of wealth and they're asking themselves, "What kind of people are we becoming?"'

*

If you walk to the end of the four blocks of apartments contained within Northcliffe, Chapelizod, you come on a doorway set low in the wall of the Phoenix Park, as in a fairy tale. Beside this is a vegetable garden where young men in navy-blue overalls are digging the ground. It is like a scene from forty years ago. Two of the young men come over to say 'Hello, hello,

hello.' They are digging potatoes with Gerald. That's Gerald over there. The young men are mentally handicapped, and are part of the day care at Stewart's Hospital.

The house in front of us, says Gerald, is Leitrim Lodge, constructed for Lord Leitrim before Phoenix Park was built. Lord Leitrim was assassinated by his tenants in the 1860s in Mohill. The house to the right of it is Drummond House, which was built as an orphanage for the daughters of soldiers and was attached to St Mary's military hospital, which still stands within the Park. The sloping site where the apartments now stand was the orchard of Drummond House. Gerald works the orphanage's vegetable garden with his team of helpers.

In a vegetable chip in a work shed he keeps all the things that they have dug up over the years. Perhaps thirty tiny thimbles; bone and iron buttons from orphanage pinafores; the china faces of little dolls whose cloth bodies have rotted away; jugs and broken cups from toy tea sets; and occasionally the clay pipes which were issued to serving soldiers. Most of these remnants are white, which makes the vegetable chip look as if it is full of children's bones.

*

Mrs Joan Finkel is an active golfer – 'I used to be a good golfer' – and a terrific driver. Leading the way in her navy Renault Clio over the blossoming motorways of Tallaght to the country road that leads to Rathfarnham, she is decisive about her lanes and a consistent indicator. She also goes at a fair clip. She used to smoke twenty cigarettes a day but gave up when she had her heart attack. She was the first female president the Dublin Progressive Jewish Congregation ever had.

Mrs Finkel and her husband John conduct funerals at the Woodtown cemetery. Together we work out how many funerals are conducted there per year. 'You're the journalist, you count,' says Mrs Finkel, scarily. Roughly 97 graves in a graveyard that has been open since 1953. Mrs Finkel takes my notepad and comes up with an average of just over two funerals per year.

Woodtown cemetery is a quiet place, the perfect hiding place. It is so quiet that to think it was very old would be an easy mistake. Its walls to the Woodtown Road are easy to climb over, and in April 1994 it was vandalized.

Twenty-six headstones were overturned and a further ten were broken. Mrs Finkel points out the crack on the headstone of one of the White boys, cousins who were killed together in a car accident in Ethiopia in the Seventies.

A TD was asked about the vandalism at the time, and implied that it was anti-Semitic. 'It was the time of *Schindler's List*,' says Mrs Finkel.

Mrs Finkel had to give the TD a piece of her mind. There was nothing anti-Semitic about it, she said. It was common or garden vandalism. When Mrs Finkel's mother died she made sure that she had a stout granite headstone which, she was assured, could not be knocked over.

The Dublin Progressive Jewish Congregation was founded in 1946 by a man called Larry Elyan, a Cork bachelor who worked as a civil servant in Dublin.

Too many religions, says Mrs Finkel, are plugged into the past. In her synagogue the women sit with the men during service. There is a mixed choir for special occasions. Young girls have a bat mitzvah at the same age that boys have a bar mitzvah. The community operates without an ordained minister. Unlike the Irish Orthodox Jewish community the progressive community is not declining. There are ninety addresses on Mrs Finkel's mailing list for the newsletter, *Menorah*, which she produces on her computer and mails herself. 'Not bad for an OAP,' says Mrs Finkel, who is sixty-seven.

The first President of DPJC was the Dublin doctor Bethel Solomons, a friend of Yeats and Gogarty. His son Michael was a gynaecologist known for his liberal views at a time when few Irish doctors, let alone gynaecologists, had liberal views. Michael Solomons was a member of the Anti-Amendment Campaign in 1983.

The DPJC bought the Woodtown graveyard because the Orthodox community wouldn't extend its burial facilities to all DPJC members. More specifically, it wouldn't bury the DPJC's converts in its graveyards. The progressive movement was outraged by this. 'As far as we're concerned, as soon as someone is admitted to Judaism the doors close behind them and they're one of us.'

Mrs Finkel pulls two pieces of chickweed out of Norman Wachman's grave as she talks.

There are small stones left on some of the graves, a Jewish custom to show that there has been a visitor. There is a grey building for prayers before the burial, these prayers consisting mainly of psalms. Kaddish is said at the graveside. 'Kaddish is a memorial for the dead that doesn't mention the dead,' says Mrs Finkel. She has heard that in the concentration camps some Jews said Kaddish for themselves, because they believed that there would be no one left alive to say it for them.

This graveyard is the place where the gang that murdered Veronica Guerin hid its guns. The gang lifted a slab that lay over one of the graves; Mrs Finkel doesn't know how they did it. She was terribly shocked when the police phoned her to tell her what had been going on. People were upset to think that their relatives' graves had been disturbed.

The Irish Times photographed and reported on the graveyard without permission – those low walls again. She was very cross about that.

Then the gardaí asked her to testify in the Paul Ward court case, to say that she would have given them permission to search the graveyard, if they had asked her.

Mrs Finkel would gladly have given it. Of the police she says, 'The left hand didn't know what the right hand was doing.'

So she spent two days in court, while the defence appealed to the Supreme Court for access to statements given against Paul Ward, and his murder trial was adjourned. (Access to the documents was denied.)

She didn't mind not being called to the witness box. 'All I would have said would have been the word "yes", twice. The only reason the guards called me was because they had to cover themselves for any eventuality.'

It annoyed her that someone like Paul Ward had someone like Patrick MacEntee acting for him. 'I mean, how much does he cost a day?' she asks. 'And who's paying for it? The tax-payer.'

She won't tell me which grave the guns and the drugs were hidden in. That wouldn't be right. 'I'm good at resisting the press. Without offence, I hope,' says Mrs Finkel.

The grave's occupant was named in court. I don't tell Mrs Finkel that.

Afterwards we go back to Mrs Finkel's house where her husband has the cricket on the television, even though he is standing in the garden. Early evening can be a sad time for those who have given up smoking.

Mrs Finkel offers me coffee, but I haven't the time.

2

[wine]

When you are touching a Prada shoe you are touching the hem of fashion. It's like holding a lot of money; you enjoy the sensation but it is a bit grotesque. I don't mean the Prada loafers, or the low-heeled slingbacks. The shoe in my hand, style number 4431, is high and pointed, with a t-strap. It is dark red, and would almost certainly make the wearer's feet look bigger and emphasize the muscles in her legs. It is a whorish shoe, the kind that female impersonators wear. It is also a triumph of engineering: the grey cross-strap is woven; the rubber heel is set in from the back of the shoe, and the rubber sole laps the upper. When you turn the shoe over the sole consists of two gentle ridges of rubber. The front of the shoe is long; the toe is almost waisted and ends in a short blunt line, like the snout of a crocodile. The long front of the low-heeled slingback is like the head of an alligator. The Italians like a little bit of brutality. The obvious is a joke to them. But to us the obvious is new, and often pretty. That's why gold Gucci mules, with gold medallions stuck on them, run out of the shops.

*

Hugh Murray is a sort of missionary. He believes in wine. He brought wine to Mullingar before Mullingar was ready for it. And soon, he hopes, he will bring Mullingar to wine, on a tour of wine-growing regions of France.

Mullingar is a stout sort of town, with prosperous Victorian streets. It used to be on the main road from Dublin to the West, a stopping-off place where you could get ice-cream cones as you went off on your holidays; only foreigners actually spent their holidays there, fishing or riding. There was always hidden wealth in Mullingar. It was a market town. Prosperous farms surrounded it, and it had a tight business community providing them with feed and machinery. But it has never been what you would call picturesque.

Now Mullingar is skirted by a motorway bypass, which was opened when Albert Reynolds, who is from nearby Longford, was Taoiseach, and it is busier than ever. Mullingar is a commuter town with jobs and traffic jams and a large middle-class population all its own. In 1996 the national census put Mullingar's population at 12,700. In 2000, according to business men who organize leaflet drops for promotional purposes, it has a population of between 16,500 and 17,000. You can feel the town burgeoning as you walk down its streets festooned with the signs of Dublin estate agents. You can see the skid-marks left by *The Irish Times* as its soaring circulation has swept through the town.

When T.P. Whelehan was a boy it was said that there were only three copies of *The Irish Times* sold here. One for Mr Black, the Church of Ireland clergyman; one for Mr Berry, the Presbyterian clergyman; and one for T.P. Whelehan's father, Kevin, who owned the chemist's. Kevin Whelehan was an unusual man: he called his sons Tom, Dick and Harry, and he sent the young Tom to the Sorbonne to complete his education. There Tom fell in with a crowd of Americans who were only too glad to educate him: 'I'd never seen boobs before in my life and suddenly I was seeing thousands of them, bobbing up and down on stage.' It was in Paris that T.P. Whelehan began drinking wine. 'My father didn't approve at all. A young fellow should be drinking pints, not have his beak stuck in a wine glass.' The young Tom later trained as a chemist, but in 1960 he started writing about wine for *The Irish Times*. He remembers that when he started there were only five wine correspondents for newspapers in these islands. 'You know what *The Irish Times* was like then. It was read by a certain type of person, and his father.' T.P. Whelehan wrote for *The Irish Times* for twenty-eight years. Now he writes for the *Sunday Independent*, and lives in Dublin.

In 1994, the year that the bypass was opened, Hugh Murray opened his first wine bar, Groucho's, on the Dublin road. He was a home boy who wanted to bring wine home to Mullingar.

'Wine is not a gift, it's an agricultural product produced by farmers for the masses,' says Hugh. He wants wine for the plain man. 'Even the *Farmers' Journal* has a wine column now.'

Groucho's served fiery chicken between two tortillas, but it was before its time. 'I started with a list of thirty wines and ended up with a list of one hundred and fifty, which was madness,' says Hugh Murray, who is in his late thirties and completely bald. The banks closed in on Groucho's.

But Hugh Murray didn't give up on wine in Mullingar. He was hired by SuperValu to organize the wine shop in their supermarket. Hugh Murray is gentle, he's interested, he is not an intimidating man. You wouldn't be afraid to ask him a stupid question. Sixty per cent of all wine in Ireland is bought by women, and at least seventy per cent of Hugh's customers in SuperValu were women who wanted advice. Let's face it, wine is a minefield. It was Hugh's male customers who wanted to cut through this minefield quickly, thinking that this would impress Hugh, underestimating the complexity of his love. It was the men who came in asking for the most expensive bottle of wine he had; it was the men who rejected bargain bottles. 'It was like that was beneath them.'

Hugh also acted as a consultant to hotels in the midlands. Hotels like the Prince of Wales in Athlone, Mullingar's great rival. The multi-nationals, like Elan and Ericsson, hit Athlone first. Hugh felt that Mullingar was not making enough of its opportunities.

When I first visited Hugh Murray in Mullingar he was just

about to open the Blue Room, a wine café in Mount Street. To this day I don't know what a wine café is, and looking round the tiny Blue Room in broad daylight it seemed a little chilly. But the Blue Room has thrived. Its customers are travel agents, teachers, accountants, and people who worked in local factories like Data Packaging, Iralco, the Malaysian company Foxteq, Mergon, the plastics factory in nearby Castlepollard, or in GMAC Commercial Mortgaging, which provides loan administration for the General Motors company.

Most of the Blue Room's customers are female. Sometimes three girls will come in and polish off three bottles of wine in half an hour – some Irish people persist in treating wine like drink – but on the whole Hugh thinks that women like wine bars because they like to talk heart to heart. Young Irish men do not enjoy this.

In the end Hugh Murray sold the Blue Room, as a going concern, to Pat Whelan, a local accountant – Mullingar is filled with accountants. Little has changed there. 'I'd say at least 80 per cent of our customers are women,' says Pat, who was once a councillor for the Progressive Democrats and is now with Fine Gael. 'It's all girlie nights out.' Some people got the idea that the Blue Room is a gay bar, so Pat is going to re-name it the Wine Café.

Hugh sold the Blue Room because he was too busy to run it. He'd been taken on as an area manager by Ecock Wines, which is run by Richard Ecock. Richard Ecock has influenced a lot of people in the Irish wine business, one of whom is Mary

Dowey, the *Irish Times* wine correspondent, to whom everyone clings as if she were a rock in a wine-dark sea. 'I had four offers,' says Hugh, 'but I went with Richard because I like his philosophy.' Hugh's own wine consultancy business has exploded. All over the midlands he trains people in how to sell and present wine. In March 2000 he ran Ireland's first wine weekend, at the Bloomfield House Hotel in Mullingar. People came from Longford, Dublin, Sligo and Cork. Then there was an eight-course gala dinner with a different wine with each course. The wine weekend was an enormous success. 'The concept was to break down barriers for ordinary people,' says Hugh. 'Somewhere between the wine grower and the customer the pomp comes in.'

Castle Street is wide enough for double parking and has the Dunne's Stores shopping centre at the end of it. This is where Bernard Smyth opened a gourmet food and wine shop called Cana. Cana's speciality is converting people to Italian wine. Bernard cannot imagine why the name Cana has never been registered before. Although the building in which Cana is housed is less than twenty years old (the premises used to be an insurance company), the interior is based on old Bordeaux wine shops. The floor is American pine. Less than a year after it opened Cana has expanded by knocking in the back office, extending the food counter and adding a confectionery section.

Bernard himself converted from being a polymer engineer to being a wine seller because he noticed that the number of professionals in Mullingar was soaring. And also because he met a woman, the sister of a beauty queen, from Bailieboro, County Cavan, on a plane back from Italy, and she was sure there was a market for Italian wines outside Dublin. This sounds like a story in a song, but Bernard is a cool customer, handsome and unsurprised. All through 1998 Bernard watched young solicitors and accountants opening their own businesses in Mullingar. He saw that Mullingar hospital was expanding. People were travelling more. Bernard knew that the person who used to drink Blue Nun and Goldener Oktober was now embarrassed by those wines. He knew that these people read the *Irish Times* every Saturday: 'Mary Dowey promotes the Italian way of living on a regular basis,' as he puts it. The Italian way of living: scooters, men who kiss each other when they're sober, and girls with very long hair. Surely it will be a struggle to get all the elements of Italian life into this country; basil is a terrible price.

Bernard looks a bit Italian already, in his sailing shoes and navy shirt. He imports wines from the Marches, the Veneto and Tuscany. There used to be a bakery, called Dusty Miller's, just opposite Cana. But that site is now occupied by Egan's opticians. Only a few years ago, Bernard says, if you had told anyone in Mullingar that you were going to open an optician's selling fancy glasses, people would have said 'Don't be raving.' But Egan's replaced Dusty Miller's and is doing very well. The Italian bread for Cana arrives, parbaked, from Delice de France in Dublin every day. Cana's brown bread is baked by local people.

It is Saturday and it has taken me hours to get here, through bank-holiday traffic. I am sweating. I stop to ask directions at the barracks, which was built in 1815. Like Athlone, Mullingar was a garrison town. It still is the home of the 4th Field Artillery Regiment. In British times regiments from different parts of the Empire would come to Mullingar to attract men into the army.

Wines Direct, by far the biggest wine enterprise in Mullingar and situated two hundred yards from the barracks, is run like a military operation, which in a way it is. Paddy Keogh was a soldier for twenty-six years. 'The wine came back to us in body bags,' he says of the early days of Wines Direct, when it was an exclusively mail-order company. His personal assistant was a quartermaster sergeant in the army. His store manager and driver is a former mess sergeant. Paddy Keogh still looks like a soldier, a neat and fit fifty-year-old with the neck of a rugby player. He is wearing a striped polo shirt. A brightly striped jumper lies over the back of his office chair. 'You have to decide whether you're going to be a general in the army, or whether to use that gene in the wine business,' he says. In the army he attained the rank of commandant, and although he is from Dublin he moved to Mullingar early in his career, because of its central location. His invasion of the wine business started in France, and only moved on to Australia last year.

Paddy Keogh has a hangover. He lost his mobile phone at a fund-raising event in the rugby club the night before and didn't get my message about being delayed. When I eventually arrived he was dealing with a young couple, so young and modestly dressed that I thought they must be brother and sister. 'They're an item,' he says when the couple leave. 'They've been touring Australia for the last eighteen months. They put their hand into every box. She said it was always worth spending on good wine.'

Paddy Keogh is that permanent stranger, a literal person in Ireland. 'The Irish tradition is verbal,' says Paddy, shaking an iron-grey head. 'They have no concept of mail order. They like to be told things, to put their hands on the thing, to have it explained to them. Don't ask them to read, they can't read. They scan things. They're like the guy in the army who will look for the signature before deciding to read the letter.'

I think guiltily of how I read newspaper articles from the bottom, and say nothing.

Paddy Keogh initially tried to move his wine by rail, but that was too expensive and too slow. 'The train service to Mullingar is a disgrace. The trains hardly go over thirty miles an hour.' It was at this time that the shattered remains of his wine came back to him in body bags; recycling the boxes in which it had originally arrived from France proved useless, because Irish people were not used to transporting wine in bulk. Eventually he designed his own box within a box and, borrowing a phrase from the Australian wine industry, had 'Handle Like Eggs' printed on the side. These boxes aroused quite a bit of interest from the older wine merchants, who wanted to know where he had acquired them. 'I said, "Sod off and get your own bloody boxes."'

Paddy Keogh likes nerve and commitment in other people. Like Eddie Walsh of Mullingar, who, says Paddy, has the finest collection of port in the country. 'He already had a pub off-licence. He dabbled in it when it was not popular. He was brave enough to go with it.'

Wines Direct delivers wine all over the country: to a restaurant on the Aran Islands, to dinner parties in Malin Head. But its customers are looking for the same thing that Hugh's ladies wanted in SuperValu, and Bernard's want in Cana: a still point in the whirling world of wine with its unfamiliar laws that make it so hard to know the right thing to do. Paddy admires people who try, who are ready to give it a go. He's there with the knowledge, the flattery, the confidence, like a preacher who came with settlers to a strange land. You want his approval. Wine experts believe that people can be educated out of virtually anything. Paddy Keogh's customers, he says, 'have got to a stage in their wine-drinking journey where they want quality. They've gone through the supermarket phase. They're a bit like yourself, successful business people' – I am still sweating in a jumper that smells like it has already been burned – 'and they entertain. Because they entertain they don't like to make mistakes. They trust us.'

Wines Direct has always had to work its way round the big companies. When finding new wine producers Paddy does two or three months' research. He visits the area, goes to the best restaurant, asks questions, sees what the local people are drinking, and tries to find undiscovered talent. 'We have to grab a guy before he becomes famous. That's hard.'

Paddy Keogh is like a villager who has learned modern ways in the big city and is coming home to dispel superstition. He understands the superstitions, but is impatient with them. He talks about the people who drink poor wine as if we were in favour of female circumcision. He is suspicious of the New World. He draws a little diagram: a cone with an X marked on it is me. There is an arrow coming from me which says Australia. 'Say you like the Chardonnays,' says Paddy. My arrow goes to Chile, then to California and then to South Africa. 'And then you might say, "What about France?" I'd say, "You're ready for France."'

The Irish fondness for New World wines is no surprise to Paddy. Until recently we were a beer-drinking and spirit-drinking nation. 'In converting beer drinkers, what they want is something fruit-driven, light. Something easy to understand. A good Bordeaux might not be palatable to the newcomer. What she'll do is go, "Yuck, I'll never drink that wine again." In fact she might not come back to French wine for a long time.' Paddy demonstrates the shock of tasting the old, the complicated, the sophisticated. 'What's that? I'm used to the hot burn of alcohol. Give me something easy.'

Now only 30 per cent of his business is mail order, and 60 per cent is with restaurants. 'One of the reasons that has developed so well is that restaurant staff are so mobile these days. They bring our name from one restaurant to another. Everybody's moving.'

A friend of Paddy's in the restaurant business was looking forward to a large party one night and afterwards told him in despair: 'It was two tables of women.' Women only drink house wine and then they want to pay separately. 'I know a woman who is earning a hundred grand a year. She goes out with her mates and they all skip starters because they're too expensive, and they won't spend more than ten pounds per head on food.'

You look at menus differently, I say, if you cook and shop for food regularly. But Paddy is still upset. 'That is a disaster for a restaurant. Worse than empty tables. And there's nothing so boring as someone on a diet. The Madison diet actually bans wine. Jesus Christ.'

There is a painting of a large Georgian house on the wall of Paddy Keogh's office. I thought it might be his home, but it is Coolmoney House, an army building in the Glen of Imaal, now demolished. 'It's a memory of all my good times there, when I was training.' He had asked for the painting when he retired from the army. 'That's what I asked for and that's what I got,' he says.

*

We have the Catholic Church to thank for New World wines. Its missionaries brought vines with them when they went to pagan countries with suitable climates. The Marists took vines with them to New Zealand, and the Benedictines brought them to Australia, part of the great missionary drive into the Pacific in the 1830s. The Franciscans brought grapes to California, and the Christian Brothers subsequently became famous for their wine there.

Altar wine can be made only from grapes: you couldn't leave Rome without it, or without the means to make it. This presented a difficulty in countries where grapes wouldn't grow. The early missionaries wrote back to Rome with queries: Could the monks in northern China use the local grapes, which grew to the size of melons? (These monks subsequently imported raisins to make altar wine.) The strainer found with the Derrynaflan Chalice, which dates from the ninth century, might have been used to strain the dregs of the altar wine, which had been diluted with elderberry wine to make it last longer.

The Church has always attached great importance to the purity of altar wine. In the Roman Missal, produced at the end of the sixteenth century, a section called 'Defects in the Celebration of Mass' states: 'If the wine has become vinegar or rotten, or has been pressed from immature or acid grapes, or so much water has been mixed with the wine so that it is corrupted, the sacrament cannot be celebrated. If the wine has begun to turn acid, or is must just pressed from it, or water is not mixed with it, then the sacrament is celebrated, but the celebrant sins greatly in doing so.'

The ruling can present problems even today. 'I remember having to deal with a priest over this,' says Monsignor McKay on the phone from Rome. Monsignor McKay, who has taken an interest in the subject of altar wine and its purity, found himself saying mass in America with a priest who had a drink problem and diluted the altar wine. 'He had so much water in it I really was worried. It depends where you stand on Alcoholics Anonymous. They say alcoholism is an illness. Other people think it is a psychological disorder, which is much less appealing. This man was acting as if any taste of wine at all would send him into an uncontrollable frenzy.'

Monsignor McKay started his research into altar wine and the process of vinification when he had an argument with a friend about must. In a church ruling on the use of altar wine, must was defined as 'wine begun and not completed'. Aborted wine, if you like. Its alcohol level is between 4 and 6 per cent.

Monsignor McKay is someone who takes the rules, and the theories behind them, seriously. He works for the Apostolic Tribunal of the Roman Rota at the Vatican. 'I'm known as the Defender of the Bond, the bond of marriage,' he says. When people apply to have their marriages annulled, 'I am paid to oppose it. I present all reasonable arguments against the granting of nullity.' Monsignor McKay, who was born in Glasgow, doesn't get his holidays until the middle of August, unheard of in the heat of a Roman summer. 'Because it is a tribunal we all have to go on holiday together. The theory was that all the judges went off in August to tend their vines.'

*

At the Red Box you stand at the side of the dance floor feeling like a Martian, your rib cage quivering to the bass line, and the only drinks you can see are five 500cl bottles of Ballygowan water and four empty cans of Red Bull cola. When you talk to people they have Red Bull on their breath, like sweet medicine. The bottles of water are two pounds each, but you can get a pint of tap water for free, in a plastic beaker filled with ice. One girl dances with an ice cube in her hand.

Tonight Renaissance, a club based in Nottingham, has arrived in Dublin. Renaissance sends its DJs, sometimes accompanied by live acts, out to clubs around the world for hundreds of gigs a year. Renaissance gigs are bi-monthly in Zurich and Moscow, and they are often seen in South Africa. It's a franchise. Renaissance has been coming to Dublin for about four years. Video screens flash up the Virgin's face from Michelangelo's Pietà, the head of David, God from the Sistine Chapel, Adam reaching out. A picture of a chrysanthemum head, lit from below, looks like a gas ring. Angels, shells, a butterfly, a group of butterflies, a sycamore leaf, photos of the models Twiggy and Loulou de Falaise from their respective youths. And photos, like postcards, of city skylines. Renaissance Singapore, Renaissance Tokyo, Renaissance Moscow, Renaissance Chicago, Renaissance Berlin. Samples and scraps.

The DJ tonight is David Seaman, who is very famous, apparently. 'I saw him in Chicago,' says Cohur, who is from Derry. 'He's intelligent. He won't fuck you round, like. He plays aggressive house.' Cohur works in a bank.

Richard used to own Bozo Fashions in the Royal Exchange in Manchester, which sold clothes by Lacoste, Paul Smith, and Henry Lloyd. Then it was blown up by the IRA in 1996. Richard had already read Tim Pat Coogan's book on the IRA before the bombing, because he wanted to know why the IRA kept on blowing things up. So he understood a little bit. Michael Heseltine, who came to see the Manchester traders after the bombing, was absolutely useless, says Richard. Michael Heseltine said that they all should have been insured against terrorist attack, but of course they weren't. Since the bombing, Richard thinks he has become much less of a workaholic. It forced him to reassess his life. Richard is forty-one. He saw the house scene turn nasty in Manchester: 'It got territorial, because of the drugs.' This is his second time in Dublin. No one turned up for his five-a-side football game on Thursday, so he drove with a mate to Anglesea in Wales, and then decided to hop on the ferry. 'I have one question,' says Richard. 'Why are there so many Spanish people in Dublin?'

David Seaman sits high over the dance floor, behind a banner with a detail from a painting of the Madonna enthroned. The Renaissance design team changes the banner periodically, and this Madonna is Miss July.

The head of David Seaman is shaved, and round like a baby's, or an alien's. David Seaman sits quietly at the turntables, he smokes a couple of cigarettes – which somehow doesn't look right – and nods to the music. He is very composed, with the passive presence of someone who is very much admired; or maybe of the permanent nightworker whose circadian rhythms are shot. His mother is a spiritualist minister. 'It's a religion. She's a clairvoyant, is my mum.'

'David, David,' says a young man afterwards. 'You're the dog's bollocks, man. You're a savage up there. You're a fucking star. I was here the other night for John Digweed. Amazing.'

David borrows my pen to sign autographs. I feel smug. 'Could you make it out to Gavin?' asks a young woman. 'He'll be so jealous I met you.'

David Seaman orders a Coke. He's wearing little black spongey shoes, Nike Air Riffs, which he says are worn by divers. The big toe is separated from the rest of the shoe, which has a strap across the foot. The shoes make you think that David's feet don't touch pavements, that he gets from one place to another by pram.

'Ecstasy,' says David Seaman, 'was the most important social development of the last two hundred years. It almost wiped out football hooliganism overnight. When I was a kid and I went to another city to hear music I had to keep my mouth shut because if they'd heard a different accent they would have killed me. Now you can go to any club in the world and be welcomed.'

David was in Amsterdam this afternoon – 'Big open-air fes-tival' – and he'll be in Ibiza for ten weeks of its thirteen-week club season. 'I suppose there has to be a focus for the music,' he says in his tired voice. 'And the focus now is the DJ. The money is crazy. I started playing records at my local youth club. I got £2.50 a night.'

Tonight is the first time that Debbie is dancing as a professional at the Red Box. 'I love it so much I'd do it for nothing,' she says. She is auditioning, for nothing, as a dancer for the Red Box, and for its sister club, the POD. Debbie comes on to the stage of the dance floor under the main video screen, wearing a hipster silver skirt and a cut-off vest top, like a Cretan bull-leaping girl. Debbie is very thin, but muscled. She never goes to the gym, she just goes clubbing three nights a week. Her stomach is a glittering cylinder of muscle. She uses her arms a lot. She drops to the floor, as if she has understood some secret message, and snakes back up, as if she's bringing back the secret. All the time smiling, not at all trying to please. A heroic dancer, who knows that she won't even be sore the next day.

Her friend Eonann is also on stage, slightly to the left of the screen, in a beige shirtwaister which makes her look as if she's just popped out from behind the photocopier. 'I'm here to make her look good,' says Eonann. 'I'm doing it for the free ticket, basically.' Eonann is from Limerick and is studying drama. 'So I'm a performer, but not in that way,' she says. Her short black hair is shining with sweat. Only the very young can look this good when they're this hot.

Up close Debbie isn't at all what you would expect. She looks like a wholesome tennis-club girl, and she talks with that sort of commonsense. 'They said if I get a good reaction, if people are looking ... that's fair enough,' she says. She works in promotions, and lives in Ballsbridge. Her parents would die if they knew she was doing this. She and Eonann are nineteen.

Someone once said that a night of dance music was like standing beside a helicopter, and that is certainly true. The music is terrible, and lovingly understood. At the Red Box tonight fringing is in, halter necks are in, straps across the back are in, strapless is in, asymmetric skirts are in, sta-prest t-shirts are in for the boys. The cloakroom is full of shiny black coats and a smattering of denim jackets. 'Guys are much more fussy,' says Cillian, who is running the cloakroom. 'They always reckon they'll lose their phones. Thirty or forty people will check in their phones and I have to listen to them ringing all night long.'

When you stick your head into the cloakroom you feel a bit dizzy, because your ears go furry in the sudden quiet.

This isn't like a dance, it's more like a religious retreat. There is no fighting, no vomiting, no lonely young men sitting it out, screwing up their courage on the bar stools. The young men are on the dance floor holding glow sticks, bouncing, dancing as if they are running. When you see a young couple kissing it seems rude somehow. This is about the group. When I ask to be brought up to the DJ, Barry, the young man in charge, who has just supervised the totting up of a what looks like a five-figure sum on the door, takes my hand to bring me through the crowd. In the Ladies there is no one crying or arguing or being sick.

Down in the POD there is an older, more familiar culture, and an older, more familiar drug – not that there were any drugs visible in Red Box. When you look at the people in the

POD, and try to imagine them elsewhere, the place you imagine them in is one of those big hospitality tents at a rich race meeting, towards the end of the day. There are more tans here, more cleavage, more matching two-pieces, more cigarettes, more anger, more drink, more worry about the notebook. The customers dancing up on stage are older (although none is over forty) and working harder to look sexy. The Irish love of dressing up, of the special occasion, is everywhere in evidence. One girl is wearing a crochet miniskirt, pink cowboy boots and a crochet bra on her tiny breasts. She looks young and old at the same time, like a page-three girl. There is bright blood on the floor of the Ladies. 'Did you cut yourself?' asks a security man through a closed door of one the cubicles. 'No,' comes the answer from the stall. 'No.'

Everyone on stage in the POD is in high heels – one woman is wearing a black bra top with floating chiffon panels, like a girl from an Austin Powers movie – except a blonde in a handkerchief top and jeans, who is calm and moving well, and Debbie, who is putting her arms out, explaining. Her feet hardly move, it's the stomach muscles that do most of the work. Come on, come on. 'The POD is much tougher,' she says. 'The Red Box is more my generation. It's harder to get people dancing in the POD.' Several of the men look as if they live in gyms, and chat to the security men. Two of them are wearing matching knitted vests, like homosexual bookends. It is in the POD that I see the only piece of clothing I recognize, a knitted dress from Karen Millen, worn by an Asian girl.

Outside, the crowds emerging from the Red Box and the POD meet. A tall tanned girl with blonde hair, a micro-mini with a lilac leather belt, a green cut-off top and a pale jeans jacket, has borrowed someone's mobile phone. She and her friend, who is wearing mauve hotpants and an orange jacket, had caused a sensation when they'd walked past the Odeon bar at the top of the street earlier this evening. She had been checking the back of her skirt then, to make sure it wasn't further up than it should have been. Now, as she hands back the phone – 'Thanks a million, I've got him to ring me back on mine' – a female voice from the Red Box crowd says, coolly, 'You've forgotten half your skirt.'

'I know, ha ha,' says the girl in the micro-mini pleasantly. Her friend, who looks exhausted and perhaps has had enough exposure for one night, says, 'Sarcastic cunt.'

'Yeah,' says the girl in the micro-mini. 'Spa.'

*

Red Bull could be the cherry cola that Lola once drank; now her grandchildren call it an energy drink. It has a metallic taste. Red Bull contains caffeine, glucoronolactone and a mysterious substance called taurine. Taurine is an amino acid. The makers of Red Bull say: 'Taurine is a conditionally essential fatty acid which naturally occurs in the body. At times of extreme physical exertion the body no longer produces the required amount of taurine, and a relative deficiency results.

Taurine acts as a metabolic transmitter and additionally has a detoxifying effect and strengthens cardiac contractility.'

Nobody knows what this means. Glucoronolactone is also said to detoxify the body. There is 80mg of caffeine in a 250ml can of Red Bull, as much as there is in a cup of filter coffee. On Red Bull's website one of the Frequently Asked Questions is this: 'I have been searching in vain in my country for a place where I can purchase Red Bull. Is there a Red Bull runway in my vicinity?' Which sounds like the innocent requests that used to come from the Eastern Bloc for denim jeans.

Red Bull was invented by an Austrian called Dietrich Mateschitz. It is claimed that Red Bull can improve concentration, enhance athletic performance, keep drivers awake on the motorway, and cure hangovers. One million cans were sold in 1987. Three hundred million were sold in 1998. Advertisements for Red Bull feature animated depictions of Adam and Eve, the cartoon priest Don Camillo, and Dracula.

*

Two years ago, says Frank, you wouldn't have had a market for this kind of thing in Cork. Frank is making me up at the Mac counter in Brown Thomas. He is wearing mascara, a good base and hint of shadow. Mac has a recycling policy, called Back To Mac, whereby you recycle their empty containers. Mac sells the nude look. Women in Cork, says Frank, like a lot of make-up. 'They'll have it on two inches thick, some of them,' he says.

'I think they want to be black people.' I say they wouldn't want to be black people in Dublin. Frank says that Cork women like dressing up to the nines. 'I don't know what kind of aristocracy we have at all,' he says. He sells me Studio Finish Satin Foundation in shade NC 35, but later I think it may be a little bit dark.

*

Hayes & Finch, a Liverpool company of candle-makers and church furnishers, shut down its Dublin factories on Bachelors' Walk in 1916 because of transport problems caused by the First World War. Some of their Dublin candle-makers went with Hayes & Finch to Liverpool. The Liverpool bottling plant, which Robert Timmons says is quite impressive – 'all spotless stainless steel' – produces 2,000 cases of altar wine per annum. 'They have quite a lot of the Anglican market, you see.'

Robert Timmons is an attractive, modern-looking man in a blue shirt. He has a moustache, two delivery vans and a four-wheel-drive car. His secretary is on holidays. 'The girl is away,' he says.

Hayes & Finch has seven branches altogether. Its Dublin branch, of which Robert Timmons is manager, is located on the Glasnevin industrial estate, where each road is called after a river. Hayes & Finch is on Barrow Road. It is very quiet here. Robert Timmons seems glad to have someone to talk to. Our conversation takes place under the gaze of a five-foot fibreglass Our Lady of Lourdes, which costs £1,700. The smaller figure of Saint Bernadette, who is looking at Our Lady across the carpet, retails at approximately £1,100.

A portable Mass kit, with silver-topped flasks to hold the water and the wine, costs £800. It is neat and luxurious and you'd take it home with you. Hayes & Finch sells four chime bells, candles, tabernacles, ciboria, tablets of charcoal (at 2p per tablet) for burning granulated incense in the thurible, lunettes for displaying the host, and special collection pouches that you can't get your hand into. The money comes out of a special locked zip at the sides.

The only thing Hayes & Finch doesn't stock is altar breads – communion wafers. 'We don't get involved because they're made by nuns,' says Robert Timmons. Hayes & Finch did not want to take away the livelihood of the enclosed orders, such as the Carmelite nuns in nearby Gracepark, who distribute their altar breads in biscuit tins. You can fit six hundred wafers into a circular biscuit tin.

Hayes & Finch sells altar vestments, which used to be made by nuns. 'There were a couple of nuns who would make you up something, but you'd be ripped off. The nuns were so expensive – we call them the little dears.'

The wine that the Hayes & Finch company distributes in Ireland comes from Provence. It is a French Muscat, near the top of the altar-wine market. It was designed for Irish and British palates. 'Some priests don't mind,' says Hayes & Finch's marketing director. 'You could give them anything and they wouldn't mind. The young guys are bit more discerning.'

Hayes & Finch's altar wine is sold at £61.50 per case, plus VAT, for twelve 75cl bottles with screw caps.

The market for altar wine increased by 20 per cent when the Catholic Church finally allowed the taking of communion under both species: bread and wine. Hayes & Finch only started advertising in the *Church of Ireland Gazette* four years ago. Since then a sizeable number of Church of Ireland clergymen have been coming to Hayes & Finch.

The Church of Ireland is rejuvenating its churches and Hayes & Finch sells its priests cloths to hang from the front of their altar. The fabric comes from France. 'For materials you can't beat the French,' says Robert Timmons.

He says of his Protestant customers, 'If you look after them they are very loyal. They'd recommend you. They're very honest.' He also deals with customers from the North, who have been driven south by the high value of Sterling.

Hayes & Finch sells solid wood benches at £40 per foot, and confessional units with screens that slide up between confessor and penitent for £300. The day of the box is over.

The church supply market is not what it used to be. 'In the Sixties it was great, there was a two-year waiting list for furniture and fittings.' Then the church building boom stopped. Now Robert Timmons doesn't think that a stand-alone church outfitter could survive in the contracted Irish market.

In the showroom is a silver and gilt monstrance that is two hundred years old and costs £6,000. Robert Timmons spends a lot of time these days rescuing the contents of convents from the clutches of pub outfitters.

I thought about the menu blackboard in one of my local pubs. It has three panels. The slogan engraved into the wooden frame reads 'Their name liveth for evermore' over the chalked list of lasagne and shepherd's pie. Naturally I would love one.

*

On Wednesday the Reverend Joseph Ojo answers his door wearing a grey clerical shirt and dog collar, a gold crucifix, and no shoes or socks. The Reverend Ojo's house is fully carpeted. It is spectacularly clean. A middle-aged Irish man is doing a little bit of painting in the kitchen. 'It didn't look good,' says Reverend Ojo, who is from Nigeria.

There is a large toy collie dog and several other children's toys in the window of the living room, where our conversation takes place. Mrs Ojo has evidently observed the importance of on-street decoration in Irish houses. Reverend Ojo's bare feet rasp as he crosses and uncrosses them from time to time.

The Reverend Ojo only became a clergyman on his arrival in Ireland eighteen months ago. In Nigeria he had been a church leader, but that's not the same thing. He was amazed to find that there was no branch of the Celestial Church of Christ in Dublin. There are up to forty branches in London alone.

Joseph Ojo was a sociology lecturer in Ondo State University in Nigeria, where he was arrested for taking part in demonstrations against military rule. His father, he says, died in prison, his brother in a car accident. 'A frame-up accident, which is very common in Africa. The moment you are against the government they are thinking how to get rid of you.'

The Reverend Ojo was escorted out of Nigeria by an Irish cleric (he had been educated by Irish priests). He knew that his bribes had worked when he was driven directly onto the tarmac at Lagos airport. After a brief stop in Paris he arrived in Dublin. 'I was very frightened but God was in control.'

Once in Dublin the Irish cleric put him in a taxi for the Department of Justice. 'That was the last time I saw him.'

I ask him how his wife felt, letting him make this dangerous journey to an unknown country. 'Oh, she and the children were with me,' says the Reverend Ojo. 'On the way she was unhappy and I had to console her.'

On Sunday the Reverend Ojo is again barefoot, and so is his whole congregation, except for myself and some children, who are in socks. The biblical justification for going without shoes in the place of worship is clearly cited on a print-out of the rules of the Celestial Church of Christ. The second item reads 'Wearing no shoes: Acts 7:33; Joshua 5:15; Exodus 3:5.'

Kelly's Row, off Dorset Street, is not an attractive place to be during a winter rain storm, or probably at any time. I had asked an old Dubliner where Kelly's Row was but, bucking the stereotype, he didn't know. It took a smart girl in a minicab office to give me the right directions from her street index.

Kelly's Row is a hymn in unrelieved concrete, with a rear view of the Hardwicke Street flats. But through the sound of windscreen wipers and the noise of the car heater the beat of an African drum and of African singing is audible.

The premises where the Celestial Church of Christ now worships were once a warehouse, and the Reverend Ojo was delighted to find them. 'God was watching over us,' he says. Earlier services had been held in the B&B he had been staying in, at Charlemont Street, soon after his arrival in Dublin. His landlord had very kindly given permission, but services soon became a bit crowded. When the Reverend Ojo moved to Leixlip the local parish priest had allowed them to use the parish hall, but the bus service to Leixlip is so bad that it was hard for worshippers to reach it from Clonsilla, Tallaght and Blanchardstown.

There are prophets amongst the believers, the Reverend Ojo says, and one of them said that their parish, which at that time had no permanent base, should be called Mountjoy parish. Shortly afterwards they found the warehouse, near Mountjoy Square. The congregation contributed £200 to buy a rich blue carpet. The shoes left in the hall are cheap.

In the main hall there are five men and five women, three little girls under ten and two toddlers. Everyone is dressed in robes of white shiny material, except a baby who is encased in a silver jumpsuit and lies quiet throughout. The women wear white satin berets on their heads. It is only when a baby girl is carried past me, wearing not only earrings but a tiny white beret placed vertically on her head, making her look like an African Child of Prague, that I remember that the Reverend Ojo had asked me to bring a scarf with which to cover my head. I wonder if I should pull up the hood of my anorak, but decide against it.

There is a man on drums, an organ and a bongo drum to the right of the altar. The choir master has not turned up. I am conscious that I reek of tobacco, and both smoking and drinking are strictly forbidden to adherents of the Celestial Church of Christ. So is 'making merry-go-round' at night, in other words wandering the streets and bars looking for members of the opposite sex. As the Reverend Ojo points out, 'We believe if you follow these rules it is very hard to sin.'

Women must undergo a cleansing ceremony each month when their period is finished. They are also forbidden from attending service with painted lips and nails. Shortly after I arrive a pretty young woman comes in with bright red lipstick and purple nail varnish – a girl who just gets on with it.

The Reverend Ojo is not very pleased with the attendance today. I am not the only latecomer. 'You must always be punctual in the house of the Lord,' he says from behind his lectern. 'Don't be disturbed by your job. Don't be disturbed by the weather. You will never be hungry because the weather is bad. These are irrelevant excuses. We must put aside lukewarmness. We must put aside getting sick every day. We're not leaving our countries because we are comfortable.

'We've come to a peaceful loving country where the hospitality is 100 per cent.' Everyone here, with the possible exception of the younger children, knows that this is a lie. A tactful lie, but a lie nonetheless. Maybe it's not a sin to tell a tactful lie.

'We mustn't forget what made us leave our countries to come to a peaceful, comfortable country.' I get a brief flash of Kelly's Row outside, and of O'Connell Street at any time of day.

'One day,' the Reverend Ojo is saying as we sit, scattered thinly amongst the twenty-four white patio chairs and looking at more chairs stacked up in the corner, 'this place will be too small. I know that. Where will you be when Jesus comes? Where will He find you? Will He find you in the pub, drinking? Will He find you making merry-go-round at night?'

I don't even have a pager.

'If you have a problem you can fast for seven days,' says Reverend Ojo. 'But when the problem is solved it's good to fast for a few hours to say thank you. It will be painless.'

'We keep living in palatial houses,' says the Reverend Ojo. 'It is good to praise the Lord.'

There is a brief song, during which everyone sings hallelujah.

The altar is three-tiered and is draped in a rich wine-coloured fabric. It has three paintings of Jesus on it, one on each level. These are local paintings; Jesus is white. There is a little tinsel around the hall and two clocks, one near the altar and one on a patio chair. There are four vases of brilliant fabric flowers.

'We must be thankful for the people who have hosted us, provided accommodation,' says the Reverend Ojo.

A young woman reads from Zachariah 10:15, on Reverend Ojo's instructions. 'He gives showers of rain. He gives comfort in rain,' she reads. I can't find this in my bible at home. Perhaps there is an African bible. The young woman is shy, and reads hesitantly. When she is finished the Reverend Ojo says, 'Sit down, my dear sister, may God bless you.' He speaks quickly in his own language. I hope he's not criticizing her reading, or talking about me.

'There are so many things that aren't right,' says the Reverend Ojo, 'that we are here to put right.' He speaks in his own language again.

The Ojos' third child, a beautiful little boy, was born after the family's arrival. The Reverend Ojo had no idea that this would allow them to stay in Ireland, he says. Now he is waiting for the documentation that will allow him to get a job, hopefully in teaching.

'This is the Bible. This is what is going to tell us the truth.' His robe has a sash with yellow fringing and three crosses embroidered on it in blue thread. The next reading is from the Book of Hebrews. 'Shall I read?' says a woman quietly. She has an educated voice. I think she might be Mrs Ojo. This reading is also about rain. 'For the earth which drinketh in the rain that cometh oft upon it, and bringeth forth herbs meet for them by whom it is dressed, receiveth blessing from God.'

'The husband is the head of the house like God is the head of the church,' says the Reverend Ojo. 'People talk of an egalitarian society, and they say that everyone is the same, that men and women can do as they like. It is not like that.'

[77]

The women's robes are wide-necked and loosely waisted.

Say someone goes astray, says Reverend Ojo. 'By the time he's arrested, by the time he's caught, everyone is saying, "Black people are criminals." We must correct ourselves. You must never take offence if a brother or sister corrects you.' Good behaviour is always noticed, it is always registered. Joseph comported himself well, and 'Joseph became second in command in a foreign place.'

A man down in the congregation takes the microphone. He has to fight feedback. 'Jehovah, thank you Lord. We want to be your children. We want to do your work but the devil won't let us do it.'

Two green buckets are passed round for two collections, and then a big brass log-box is carried forward by the men. The drummer starts again and the congregation sings 'Pay your tithes everybody, do not delay, tomorrow may be too late, pay your tithes, pay your tithes ...'

Two trays of offerings are brought up. One by a man, on which there are candles, and one by a woman, on which there is sugar, honey and salt. Then everyone dances, step, step, in place. I smile tightly.

Everyone praises the Lord. 'Thank you, Lord,' says Reverend Ojo. Oh yes, says the congregation. The Reverend Ojo thanks God for me. 'She has come to worship with us,' he says. I feel bad about writing in my notebook.

We turn to the north, south, east, and west and say seven hallelujahs and seven hosannas and seven ebenezers to each point of the compass. Twice. I am always facing in the wrong direction. (Later the Reverend Ojo explains that Ebenezer is another name for Christ.) We sing the Our Father – a yellow maraca has to be taken from a tiny boy. 'Bless us going out,' says the Reverend Ojo, as the congregation disperses to its respective homes in Clonsilla, Tallaght, Leixlip, James' Street.

After the service Wole Saidu, who works as a security guard at a computer plant, explains that the Celestial Church of Christ was founded in Nigeria in 1947, 'when they were having a lot of satanic problems'.

People's Christian faith was weak at that time, he says. 'Say I am a Christian, say you are a Satanic practitioner ...'

'For example,' I say quickly.

Curses were put on people by satanic practitioners, 'that you would never be successful, or could never have children – something awful. Many people went down, they got very depress,' he says. The Celestial Church of Christ was set up to counteract this worrying phenomenon with vigorous Christianity.

'Say you are on the seventh day or the eighth day of your cycle,' says Mr Saidu in a friendly way. 'Then when you come to service you bring a candle and a sponge, which are prayed over, and you are cleansed. If you had been here earlier you would have seen it.'

My own mother was churched after giving birth to me, I say.

Yes, yes, say Mr Waidu and the Reverend Ojo. 'Forty days, forty days.'

After the blood is gone, presumably.

Edited transcript of interview on *Today with Pat Kenny*, RTÉ Radio One, 25 November 1999, 10 a.m.:

Pat Kenny: All sorts of very interesting things to bring you in the programme today.

But we're starting by harking back to the conviction of James Kelly, known as Brother Ambrose, who worked at Lota, a home for disadvantaged children run by the Brothers of Charity in Cork. As you know, James Kelly received the longest-ever jail sentence for sex-abuse offences – thirty-six years in all. His conviction closes a chapter in an intensive Garda investigation which actually began six years ago. Sergeant Senan Ryan from Glanmire in Cork led the investigation and he's on the line. Sergeant Ryan, good morning.

SR: Good morning, Pat.

PK: And first of all, I have to say congratulations. It was an investigation which went on a long time and I'm sure was fraught with many difficulties.

SR: It was indeed. It was a very difficult and traumatic investigation, both for myself and for the other members with me at the time.

PK: You were the garda at the very beginning of this. Can you remember what prompted the investigation, the single incident?

SR: Well the single incident that happened, it happened on

the ninth of the eleventh of '95, when an individual from the north Cork area came into the station. He had called apparently three or four times before that but couldn't pick up the courage to come inside the door. When he eventually did he asked to see me and he ... in confidence, and ...

PK: Did he ask to see you by name, by the way?

SR: Eh, no. He was aware that the Glanmire area and Lota were covered by the Glanmire garda station.

PK: OK. So he could have got someone sympathetic or otherwise, he didn't know. He was putting his faith in the Garda Siochána.

SR: He was just putting his faith in the Garda Siochána and the reason he came to Glanmire was that he was aware that the gardaí in Glanmire used call to Lota many years ago as well, and that they'd pass the station here when they would be out for walks.

PK: So he passed up and down outside the station four, five, six times maybe before plucking up the courage to come in?

SR: That is correct.

PK: What did he tell you?

SR: [*Deep breath*] Well, when he came in I asked him to sit down. We went to a private room and he told me to sit down, or he asked me to sit down, because he said 'I have something horrendous to tell you', and they were his first words. And he sat there for at least ten minutes before he spoke a word. Couldn't talk. And eventually he started to talk and he couldn't be stopped. It poured out. Eh, I was on my own at the time and I just left him talk. I didn't take notes, I didn't record anything, and when he had finished I said that we will call to him within a week or so, when I'd have another member with me and take a detailed statement from him.

PK: What was your reaction to hearing some of the very graphic detail of the chronicle of abuse that had happened to this man? I mean were you shocked, were you surprised, or had you had any suspicions?

SR: Eh, no. I had no suspicions at all that there was anything going on, or anything had gone on in Lota at that time. I never got a complaint as such, and I was shocked. His story was unbelievable, to say the truth. I mean it was the truth but it was so unbelievable to believe that such a thing could happen at that time.

PK: Yeah. I mean in, for example, the Dublin area, people would have heard things about Artane. There would have been rumours going round and about, not so much about sexual abuse but certainly about extreme physical abuse of children. Certainly in my childhood you were threatened with Artane. Now Lota was never seen as that kind of place in your childhood, was it?

SR: No, and I'm from, I come from Limerick, and I didn't even know Lota existed until I came to Cork.

PK: So there would have been no rumour machine around the place, saying it was an awful place, or anything like that, when you came to Glanmire?

SR: No. No. Nothing about Lota until the end of 1995.

PK: So, your reaction hearing this. I mean, was it disbelief first of all, or did you find your witness so credible that, in spite of the incredible nature of what he was saying, you felt constrained to believe him?

SR: Yes, I know he was so hurt. And he cried so much, he cried unbelievable with me. I knew he was telling the truth, and it wasn't a make-believe situation. That he was telling the truth. And, as I said, I believed it so much that I organized notes and went up to his hometown where we met him, in confidence, without the local gardaí knowing in that area as well, because that's what he wanted.

PK: Yeah, and how long did it take to take detailed statements from him?

SR: Eh, it's the longest statement I ever took, timewise. It took approximately seven hours, as the man broke down on several occasions during the statement. It was just, to see a grown man cry while the statement was being taken had a fierce effect on the two of us there that day.

PK: How therapeutic was it for him to talk to you, because he'd obviously bottled this up for years, and suffered from it?

SR: Eh, when the statement was finally finished and we had, after several cups of tea and cups of coffee and cigarettes during the day, he felt great. He felt great, and before we left that day he caught a grip on my hand to say goodbye to me, but it wasn't to shake hands, the grip was so, eh, tight that I thought he'd never let go of my hand. And I'll always remember that. [*Deep breath*]

[...] PK: And one man's evidence alone might not be enough to convince the DPP that terrible things went on in Lota. So you had to find other people.

SR: Eh, yeah. Though we didn't canvas, and we couldn't canvas for victims. But when we made discreet enquiries from the names we were given by this man from north Cork, that were with him during that time, the calls started to come in, and we picked it up from there. We had to visit these people's towns and villages round Galway, Limerick, Tipperary ...

PK: And you made a decision that you would do this yourselves, that to preserve the confidentiality of the investigation you didn't want local gardaí from those areas making the enquiries.

SR: That was everyone's wishes. They did not want local gardaí because they were living still in rural Ireland, they were very familiar with their local gardaí and they could meet their local gardaí walking the street, and they were able to say 'Hello Tom, hello Michael, how are you', and they wanted to continue that without knowing that the local gardaí knew of the past. And that's the reason that we decided that we would visit these towns and villages around the country.

PK: You got a chronicle of gross physical and sexual abuse, and in court the judge described it as a crucifixion for these, as they were then, children.

SR: Yes, and that's what it was, yes.

PK: And that's what it was.

SR: Yes. ... And there was a conviction there in relation to the first victim that came into the station, with others.

PK: Yeah, and this was a different brother involved than James Kelly who was convicted the other day?

SR: It was, yeah. It was.

[...] PK: Was there ever any attempt to persuade you not to proceed with the prosecution because of the age of James Kelly?

SR: You see, Pat, this happened so long ago. The people it happened to were eleven, twelve, thirteen at the time. [...] And now I was dealing with them, they were mid-forties and they remember their abuser as a mid-thirty-year-old man that gave them hell, and that's what happened. Like, you know, he gave them hell. And they remember him at that age. But when I was investigating I had the victims and their stories that they told me were unbelievable, it, it, it, it ... unreal. But then as a result of that I had to interview an eighty, seventy-nine, seventy-six-year-old man. Feeble, not well, fierce timid, fierce nice person to speak to, butter wouldn't melt in his mouth. That's the impression that he would give at the interview. 'Twas hard to picture the material that I had before me, and the material that I had to put to him, it's hard to believe that such a thing could happen.

[...] And I had to deal with the victim professionally. Likewise, I had to deal with the culprit professionally. And during the interview with the culprit I saw him, what he was now. And I had to interview him accordingly as to what he did in the late Fifties, early Sixties. And 'twas difficult, very difficult.

PK: But my question, was there any attempt to persuade you that this man was too old?

SR: No. No.

PK: And that therefore should not face the full vigour of the law?

SR: No. No. No, definitely not, and as Judge Murphy said in court, terrible crimes were committed at a time when the society had an inability to face up to the enormity of them. And now society has. And I think it should ...

[...] PK: Did you expect to have a long and fairly harrowing case on your hands going through the courts to secure a conviction?

SR: Up to two days before the court I was led to believe that there would be a plea of not guilty. But two days before the court I was informed that there was going to be a plea of guilty. I had brought witnesses over from England – they were now living in Scotland, sorry – and from Dublin, and Wexford. And two days before the court, a plea of guilty was put forward.

PK: And this was of huge relief to all the victims who were prepared to give evidence.

SR: It was huge relief, because if they had to say what I have taken in statements you know it's un, it's un, it's unbelievable. It's unbelievable.

PK: What impact has this investigation had on you?

SR: Well, you know, you must remember there are gardaí all over the country doing this type of investigation now.

PK: I know.

[86]

SR: On me, it had an impact on, on, on me. You think about it a lot. Em, the gruesome details. Taking statements from people over a five, six, seven-hour period. Sitting down in a room with them crying. Yes it has. It had a terrible effect on me, yes.

PK: Could you characterize the victims of that abuse in any way? You've met a number of them, quite a number of them. Do they have anything in common?

SR: They do. They were placed, because for whatever reason, either they were orphans, or their time, or because it was decided that they needed special education, and that the local schools couldn't cater for them, and their parents couldn't look after them, they were placed in Lota, in the care of the Brothers of Charity. They have all that in common.

[...] PK: And what about the silence of those good brothers who didn't feel they could speak out?

SR: Well, evil prevails when people stay silent. When good people stay silent, I suppose.

PK: Yeah.

SR: And that's what we have to think about.

PK: Well, your work obviously continues on other crimes, but I'm sure you're glad to have the file closed on this one.

SR: I am, yes. I am. I am.

PK: Thank you very much, Sergeant Senan Ryan, and once again, congratulations to you and your colleagues.

SR: Thank you, Pat. Thank you.

John walked straight into the boom. 'I felt that good sense when I came out, and I felt I could get it. There wasn't a depressed atmosphere. There was a buzz about it. Hope for anybody who wanted to take it. I remember all the cranes. It was just amazing. To walk in the Financial Services Centre and to see a pub there. I didn't feel any envy or want to be part of it at all. There was more fun, it was most striking. I walked all over the city. I walked and walked and walked. I noticed that while people put more emphasis on labels, that they didn't seem so well dressed. Everything was more casual. I saw that women had really advanced, in their financial position and in their independence. I saw them out together, in groups, and drinking pints of course. The cars! I just thought, isn't it just as well I don't have one, or don't have a family that would need me to have one. Not having children of my own felt very, very painful when I was younger, but it's a blessed relief now.'

John had served a long prison sentence for the sexual abuse of teenage boys below the age of consent. 'I can't tell you what prison smells like. I lost my sense of smell, with the shock of the whole thing.'

John was a priest and technically still is. I cannot describe him, in case a description might help to identify him, and thus his victims. This is a pity, because John is a lively and vivid man and a fluent, unflinching talker. Likeable. He has the glow of someone who has found an explanation for something that had mystified and tortured him for years.

When John was walking around the new Dublin he was consumed with shame. He felt as if he had a mark on him, on his front and on his back, like the mark of Cain. He thought everyone knew where he'd been, and why. 'I had to learn to live every day with the horror of what I had done. That's always there, but it has to be with all the other things. It's not a "poor me" thing, it's just an everyday thing. And you know I wouldn't be without that, or I could slip into denial again. There are painful realities in life which keep you on track.'

John was in therapy for a long time, and speaks without embarrassment about his inner child. I say that I think confession was the greatest invention of the Catholic Church. John says, 'It was the only therapy there was in those days, Ann Marie.' John believes in therapy, which has shifted his sexual interest away from teenagers, towards adults.

'It started off with touching, Ann Marie, and progressed to the whole thing.' These relationships were couched in romantic terms, and declarations of love were exchanged. 'Although it was always me asking the question.'

John was obsessed. At the end he wouldn't go out of the house where he lived anymore, in case a boy would ring. At the end, he says, he was suicidal. He tried to persuade the boys that what was happening was perfectly normal. The physical relationships involved penetration, both by him and of him. At all times John encouraged the boys to believe that what was happening was normal and would not affect their relationships with young girls, something he also encouraged. John will talk about all this, although he becomes distressed when doing so. He's talked about it in therapy. They didn't talk about God often in his therapy group, which contained other clerics, as well as lay-men. 'Sometimes. Not much. The reason was that lots of us used God, in terms of going to confession and getting absolution, telling the sin in the vaguest terms. I believe in God now very much in my own way. It could be a woman now, for all I care. God, it's a being, it's a meditation, it's quiet, it's listening, it's within myself.'

John still goes to Mass. But he would not say Mass. 'No. I would feel that what I did to the priesthood and to the Church, I wouldn't feel entitled to say Mass. I wouldn't put myself forward. I would find the fantasy of vesting, of going in front of people – my skin would crawl, Ann Marie. That's just me. There's plenty of others who do. I don't find it hard, I find it true. It is my choice.'

He had been a model prisoner, as most child-sex abusers are. The first morning he was in Mountjoy an officer called out 'Good morning, Father,' as the prisoners assembled. In any event, John had been expecting cruelty. 'It was the kindness I felt the most, I was expecting rejection. An unexpected kindness from a prisoner or an officer would reduce me to tears. The prisoners made hooch one Christmas out of orange juice and bread. They soak the bread for the yeast. I had one sip of it.' He throws his eyes up to heaven. 'That was a laugh, actually.'

We meet at my house. It's the first time I have ever interviewed anyone in my home. I apologize for the kitchen, which used to be two rooms until we knocked down a wall. It has been awaiting redecoration for over a year, and is pretty shabby. 'Oh no,' says John. 'You've let the light in.'

The right thing to say. A man who has had a lifetime of visiting other people's houses.

3

[water]

They say that the yacht clubs have changed, but it's hard to say how. Yacht clubs have a way of making you feel foreign, even if you grew up on their doorstep and in their social catchment area. To be the member of an Irish yacht club is to have reached safe harbour; or to have been born into one. In a safe harbour you are guaranteed that the sea of money will never fall below a certain level. The Ansbacher boys, owners of secret and illegal offshore accounts, wear sailing shoes with their lemon v-neck sweaters during their leisure hours. When I think about the Dún Laoghaire yacht clubs I think of wet summer nights and a halter-necked evening dress I wore with high espadrilles. Uncomfortable in every sense. Early youth.

It is regatta day and pouring rain. They haven't put the chairs or tables out in the marquee yet, and the canvas walls look sodden. All those dreary discos. There is an electronic security system on the front door. And on the basement door, which was presumably once the tradesmen's entrance. There are more big white fibreglass boats in the harbour than there used to be. Many of the biggest yachts are over in Howth, where, they say, there are better sailors and better racing. Howth's marina encourages bigger boats. Dún Laoghaire is now building a marina of its own.

A big man with a red face is putting too much diesel in the tank of his boat, and the fuel, which looks green and soapy, is overflowing and splashing over the side and into the water. 'She has enough, she has enough,' shouts one of the boatmen in alarm. In the bar there are more navy sweaters than you thought existed outside Spain.

'Oh, it's insurance brokers and the new rich,' says a woman despairingly. 'And the food is so appalling. It's chequebook sailing now.'

The British came on the first tide. Then it was the Irish lords and retired majors. Then it was the Dublin bourgeoisie: doctors, lawyers and businessmen who knew how to hold their knives. Every time a new tide comes people feel that Atlantis is being swept away. Old money has always looked down on new money, and in Ireland almost all money is new. So there is a waterfall of disapproval for the new rich and even the newly prosperous, which starts slowly amongst the oldest money of all, now nearly gone, and then flows over the more recent arrivals, until it is a torrent of disdain.

'They had to let them in,' said one old yacht club servant darkly. 'The Royal Cork nearly went under because it tried to keep them out.'

'Too posh,' I say helpfully.

'Not too posh,' he says in disgust. 'Decent people. Gentle-men. People who had manners and knew how to talk to you.' He's referring to the lords and to the retired majors. Not to the Irish bourgeoisie, which has the sort of social confidence that doesn't so much hide shyness, ineptitude or despair, as give us a ten-second start.

There are three old yacht clubs in Dún Laoghaire. The Irish was, in the opinion of the old guard, the last to be spoiled. 'That's because they kept out the Catholics for a long time,' says a Catholic. 'They were the last to let in ladies. They still have black-balling in the Irish.'

Prods in the Irish, rich Catholics in the George and fun peo-ple in the Nasher (the National), or so they say. There used to be talk of wife-swapping down in the Nasher, which was always regarded as the gas club, more gutty than the rest. But that was in the old days.

Even children's sailing is crowded now. There is a circuit of junior regattas in yacht clubs round the country, and the chil-dren are transported between them. 'You have sailing moth-ers. They're obsessive. It's like the pony set.' The yacht clubs are putting a lot of energy into running training courses for children; one employee called these courses 'the most expen-sive baby-sitting service in the world'.

There is more money, but less time. The Friday lunches in the yacht clubs are now almost deserted, where once people would linger drinking port for the rest of the day.

There was always sailing on Thursday evenings and on Saturday. On Thursday evenings nice young men would tear off their ties, delighted to leave the office early and go out to crew on a big boat that belonged to someone else. It wasn't a late night, but it was a pleasant one. Now it's increasingly difficult to find anyone to do this.

'Thursdays are gone,' said an old member. 'Nobody is going out anymore, they're all working so hard. They go on campaigns but they cut out the fun part. They can't leave the office to slobber round Dún Laoghaire bay.' And then there's the traffic out of town.

There are also many pavilion members, who never sail at all, whose companies are thought to have paid their subscriptions. But how can you tell?

In the George they serve hamburgers downstairs. 'It's a business now,' said the boatman. No one can name what it was before, and I can't myself. An island, perhaps.

*

Looking back it seems to have been always raining in the Seventies. We never had raincoats then, we wore fur coats and Afghan jackets that smelled like meat when wet. Rain made wearing clogs particularly difficult. Your bare wet feet kept slipping out of them. Clothes were thin – fashionable jumpers were made of nylon – and so we were often cold. Sodden denim did not dry in front of the gas fires in our bedsits and flats, which were damp no matter what the weather. The boys had to mop their long hair with striped towels. It was an uncomfortable time.

Irish people are the ones who never wear raincoats. We don't like planning and we don't like reality. In fact, the total rainfall in Ireland in the 1990s was higher than it was in the 1980s, and considerably higher than it was in the 1970s. At the weather station in Belmullet, County Mayo, they recorded 10,749 millimetres of rainfall in the 1970s, and 12,871 in the 1990s. The Casement Aerodrome near Dublin city recorded a total rainfall of 6,695 millimetres in the 1970s and 7,480 millimetres in the 1990s. All I can say is that doesn't feel like that. Perhaps the extra rain falls at night. It feels as if the nature of the rain has itself has changed, with fewer of the fine mists that silently drenched you, and more tropical downpours. Niall at Met Éireann says it seems like that to him, too, but there is no research available on the changing nature of rain. Memories are unreliable.

*

St John's Wort has stopped a lot of tears; or maybe started them, it depends on your point of view. St John's Wort contains *hypericum perforatum*, which is thought to be an antidepressant. Like Rescue Remedy, St John's Wort is a name that has emerged from the world of alternative health and now bobs in the mainstream. You can buy St John's Wort candles.

Tony & Tina add St John's Wort to their Mood Balance Lipstick. But Tony & Tina's products are not yet available here.

On 28 August 1999, St John's Wort was banned by the Irish Medicines Board because it feared that *hypericum* caused photosensitivity, and could react badly with other medication, such as prescribed anti-depressants, over-the-counter cough medicines, the contraceptive pill and Warfarin. The Irish Association of Healthfood Stores was officially informed a couple of days later. The ban took effect on 1 January 2000.

'At that stage I was free-floating, doing promotional work for someone who does t'ai chi. We were all, "Oh my God, what are we going to do?" St John's Wort was the second highest selling herb in the country after echinacea.'

Gabrielle McCauley is a thin woman in her fifties with a long skirt and long earrings. She lives in Tallaght. She has a coffin in her garden shed. It is a cardboard coffin, about four feet long and stapled along its base. 'It's just perfect,' she says. On the coffin is a piece of paper that reads 'St John's Wort RIP 01012000.'

Gabrielle was the chair of the campaign that was formed to fight the banning of St John's Wort. She worked in the first health-food store in the Square shopping centre in Tallaght. Now there are three health-food stores there, one on each floor.

'Women precipitated that movement. Tallaght had a huge problem in the past with tranquillizers. Women wanted something that was not addictive. People became disillusioned with conventional medicine.'

Ginkgo biloba, which is thought to ward off Alzheimer's disease, and to help with peripheral circulation problems, was banned at the same time as St John's Wort. 'The oldest tree in the world,' says Gabrielle sadly of *Ginkgo biloba*. 'And a herb that is so wise that it only blooms on St John's Day. The nerve, the cheek, the audacity of it.'

Gabrielle knows her market. 'William Morris wallpaper became fashionable as people in Britain moved off the land and into the cities.' She has watched alternative health remedies enter the mainstream. The male executive now, she says, will use tea tree oil for his athlete's foot and lavender oil in his bath, without thinking twice about it.

Gabrielle believes that people are more depressed now than they have ever been. She knows that from talking to them: 'We're lonely in the cities.' Gabrielle is from Oranmore in County Galway, where her mother is still the postmistress.

For many years health-food shops were not busy. Now they are booming, but the old culture, of assistants standing in quiet health-food shops, ready to talk, has persisted. Gabrielle is not at all surprised that total strangers would walk into a shop and tell the assistant that they are depressed. Only they don't say that. They say that they're feeling a bit down.

'St John's Wort is for when you're just a bit blue, just a bit down. Very often, if it's a man, they won't go to a doctor but their partner can nip in and pick up something in a health store.'

In a written response to a question put down in the Dáil on

14 June 2000, six months after the banning of St John's Wort, the Irish Medicines Board's view on this sort of practice was read into the record. 'The Board had expressed concern at the possible treatment of mild moderate depression by use of an over-the-counter medicine. The Board considers that the treatment of such a condition should be under medical supervision and that self-diagnosis and self-medication are inappropriate.'

Just walking into a health-food shop can make a person feel better. 'People love the photos on the boxes, particularly on the herbals. They like to see the flowers. The photos are really important. Some Bach flower remedy experts, they say you don't have to take the remedies. You just have to look at the photos.'

Gabrielle has worked in health-food shops and for natural-remedy wholesalers since her eldest son, Conor, was a baby. 'He had had six courses of antibiotics in ten months, so I went to a naturopath. I felt very, very lonely and isolated at the start.' Conor is twenty-three now and has recently been recruited by Motorola. 'In a year he'll be earning more than I do,' says Gabrielle.

The whole St John's Wort campaign, which is known as the SJW campaign for short, was very tiring. 'I just used to get into bed and take the phone off the hook. I was going to sleep thinking campaign, waking up thinking campaign. I was thinking, if this herb is banned, what are our children going to do? They're going to have to take drugs.'

Now when people need St John's Wort they order it off the

Internet, or they go North, often to a health-food store in Newry. It may even be illegal to tell people about these sources. 'It's like abortion referral,' says Erica of the Hopsack health-food store in Rathmines shopping centre. 'But I had a run of menopausal women today, and what could I do?'

In January 2000 two Green TDs, Trevor Sargent and John Gormley, brought St John's Wort down to Dublin on the Belfast train, just as contraceptives were brought down from Northern Ireland in 1971. These are the activists. In the wings stand the big pharmacists and supermarkets, the biggest sellers now of herbal remedies – just as the GPs took to handing out contraception without once having pounded a pavement.

Someone is doing a thesis on whether there was a misogynistic element in the banning of St John's Wort. Gabrielle has absolutely no doubt that there was. 'I think the whole natural health movement parallels the women's movement and women not going to church so much anymore. I mean, why choose St John's Wort, the herb for depression? Why did the government choose that herb?'

She has never taken St John's Wort in her life. She waves a hand towards a shelf of pills and tinctures in the corner of her kitchen, and there's a photograph of an elderly couple placed next to it. 'It's a feng shui bagwa. That's where you acknowledge your ancestors.' Gabrielle's grandparents had a beautiful garden. That's where she first learned about flowers and herbs. Wind chimes hang by her back door. I must get wind chimes for my own back door, which the feng shui lady said was too closely aligned with my front door. Life is full of things you have to do.

The coffin in Gabrielle's garden shed was used at a wake for St John's Wort, a protest march that proceeded from the Irish Medicines Board's office in Earlsfort Terrace to the Dáil. 'We would have loved a grand march, but I knew there wasn't a hope in hell. Our main difficulty was in getting people to turn up to things.' People don't participate in voluntary campaigns anymore, and contributions to them are falling. Gabrielle spoke to Clare Watson of the campaign against genetically modified foods, and she said exactly the same thing. 'People are so busy, so stressed out, they haven't time.'

The SJW campaign was run through the health-food stores, and it was through this network that it collected 65,000 signatures for its petition to the Minister for Health. It also urged people to write to their local TDs objecting to the banning of SJW. And they did. In the end, says Gabrielle, the banning of St John's Wort may have been a blessing in disguise, because now it looks as if the alternative health sector will get some system of regulation, which Gabrielle believes has been badly needed for years.

At one point the SJW campaign was thinking of running a candidate in the next general election. But then Brian Cowen, who had been Minster for Health during the banning, was moved to Foreign Affairs in February, and there was talk that Micheál Martin would succeed him. Micheál Martin was appointed Minister for Health on a Thursday and on the Saturday morning Breda Dooley, Gabrielle's successor as chair of the SJW campaign, was sitting in his constituency clinic in Cork. 'Breda is a user, she's a German-speaker and she used to work with Tom O'Donnell in Europe. We had heard that if you can get into the Minister's backyard you can move things, because his own seat is at stake. I do hope they don't have to campaign in Micheál Martin's constituency. I think he's a nice man.'

*

A power shower is to rid you of stress, rather than grime, although you do feel unassailably clean afterwards. Nothing could withstand that onslaught of water. The power shower drives all thoughts from your head. You cannot concentrate on anything but the water falling. The power shower is for the morning. You stumble in a bleary invertebrate and you bounce out ready to kill. It's like standing in your own private typhoon, and you can switch the dial to 'boost' if things get a bit slow.

*

The road gets rougher as you approach the well and my friends dropped me at the end of it, because they weren't going to risk their new Alfa Romeo on what, after you pass the building sites that surround the new houses, becomes a rough boreen. It has been out of use since the 1930s, when the county council chose other roads to cover with tar. Some of the new houses are in an estate called Dún Eoin. At least they're calling them something local. In Sandymount there is an apartment block called Radclyffe Hall. In Leixlip there's a housing estate that used to be called Cyber Plains, before the county council insisted on a change. It's the Aylesburys and the Chesterfields and the San Lorenzos you feel sorry for.

You can hear the rosary as you approach. The road slopes down, and to the left of it, in a clearing of trees, is a crowd of about seventy people. You know you're in County Cork because women turn to you to say hello. Three old ladies are sitting on one of the stout benches, and five white-haired men are standing in kilts – the Carrigaline Pipe Band. 'At the height of their achievements they won Intermediate Grade Two in Munster,' a man says later.

Canon O'Brien is also white-haired, standing behind the gold sunburst which contains the Host. It's the brightest colour here, except for the fluorescent pink hair-ties that hold a little girl's pigtails in place.

Novartis, a pharmaceutical company, put in the railway sleepers which serve as steps, and the benches for the old ladies. The company has a plant in nearby Ringaskiddy. Novartis used to be called Sandoz. 'They had a bit of a spillage there a couple of years back, in Berne,' says Seán O'Mahony, who used to work for Telecom before he retired and became a local historian.

The developer of the new houses cleaned the area up and

put down grass seed. 'Stephen,' says Michael Wall sharply, once the prayers are over. 'I'll kill you, cycling over the new grass.' Michael Wall is praised in Canon O'Brien's closing remarks for his part in getting Saint Ronóg's well designated a Protected Shrine in the new County Development Plan. There is applause.

Michael Wall moved to the nearby Carrigcourt estate fourteen years ago, and fell in love with the well. 'I come up here on my own most mornings. There are two robins who live here and they sit down beside you. I maintain it and keep it weed-free. It's a little bit hard to explain it. I take away the rubbish and say a prayer. I don't say the rosary. I just say it my own way.'

Michael Wall is a big bald man in a sports shirt with a logo. 'People come here in the early mornings. There's a steady flow and they do their own passions, the five crosses. Oh, it is lovely. Round the well usually three times or maybe five. They come for special intentions, or if someone is sick.'

You can look down on Saint Ronóg's well from the steps. You walk around the well and recite a decade of the rosary at each of the five crosses set into the wall of the beehive. Tonight the Canon gave a little sermon at the end of the rosary. Mothers crouch down beside buggies; the older children are playing in a subdued way in the trees. This is a pattern, a celebration of the patron saint. The patron saint of Carrigaline is John the Baptist, and this is Saint John's Eve. St John was once celebrated all over the country – 'it was on the twenty-third of June, the day before the fair'.

The band goes into a military drum-roll as Canon O'Brien holds up the Blessed Sacrament. Then he takes a vessel of well-water and a green fern and with it splashes a section of the crowd in turn. He walks around the clearing to do this, coming up the steps to us. He's smiling as he does this – Canon O'Brien is a rational man – and we smile as the water splashes onto us, and each person crosses himself with the tiny sign of the habitual churchgoer. Religion feels different outdoors. The band plays 'Amazing Grace'.

When Canon O'Brien genuflects, his knee doesn't touch the ground. He has arthritis, like many former athletes in old age. He used to train the Cork hurling team. He is a character.

Saint Ronóg's well is one of the few in Ireland that has a beehive covering. Nobody knows how old the well is. 'They say the nearest thing like it is on the Skelligs,' says Seán. Behind us is what used to be called the Tent Field. Mass was said there last year, but now there are the skeletons of new houses on it.

'It was the worst crowd we ever had tonight,' says Michael Wall. 'I would say seventy or eighty people. But the wife of a man in the parish died, and there's a rosary for her tonight at eight o'clock down at the funeral home. He's involved in the Community Association.'

'And in the twinning as well,' says Seán O'Mahony.

'So a lot of people would have gone to that, you see, instead of here.'

This is Canon O'Brien's fifteenth pattern and he disagrees about the numbers, although he allows that they were relatively thin. 'I could see through the crowd tonight. But it wouldn't be short of 150, whereas normally it would be about 300. There were no Ballinahassig people tonight.' Seán and Michael listen to this estimate, which entirely contradicts their own, and everyone else's, in polite silence.

Inside the well you have to crouch a little and step over stones to reach the stream itself. 'Go round the ledge on the side,' says Michael. There is a shelf on the back wall, on which stands a single card with a picture of the Virgin. 'People used to leave written prayers here, but not lately. Or if they are praying for someone they leave something belonging to the person, or to themselves.' It is almost pitch black in here.

'I am amazed, because normally today it is full of candles,' says Michael. He and Seán talk for a moment about who normally brings candles on this day.

Twenty-five years ago there was an ash tree growing out of the well, and the whole thing was on the point of collapse. The council removed the tree and, for the first time, added mortar to the stones. The water has never been tested.

The well is thought to be particularly powerful in helping blind people, and in his sermon Canon O'Brien had mentioned a blind man who was cured at the well. Blind people used to come here and say the rosary while passing a pebble between them. At the end of each decade whoever had the pebble would trace the line of the cross with it.

In the last century the pattern lasted seven days, from tonight, the 23rd, to Saint Peter and Paul's day, on the 29th. It was one of the biggest patterns in Munster. 'The festival was commercialized,' says Seán. 'They'd set out stalls selling religious objects. There was a fair, where they were said to sell everything from a needle to an anchor. Unfortunately, there was a lot of drinking went on. I always say that the people had hard lives then and that the drinking was partly to drown their sorrows. I say that now as a non-drinker.'

I say drinking is always partly to drown your sorrows. And I say that as a drinker.

In all his researching of the well, Seán says, 'I have no positive proof or reference as to a cure.'

By 1843 there was no drinking at the pattern. 'They got a much smaller crowd.' Seán has all this information in an old copybook, written in red and green ink. These are the notes for a lecture he has given on the subject. He holds out the cover of the copybook towards Mary. 'What year is on that?' he asks. He hasn't got the right glasses with him.

'Ninety-six,' she says, as we walk back to the car, all wearing jackets. Mary and I are freezing. 'Last year we were rained out,' she says. We go back to Seán and Mary's house for tea.

One of their sons, Seamus, works for Pollution Control Systems in Ringaskiddy. It's used mainly by the dairy and pharmaceutical industries. About 20 per cent of its business is in Ireland, where it employs twenty people. 'The entire company, this is it,' says Seamus. An Irish man bought the company in Norway, improved quality control and moved it here. Seamus's little daughter wanders round the kitchen where Seán

and I are talking, where the Sacred Heart hangs over the television, with the Father's Day cards marshalled in between. The
kettle sits on the Rayburn stove.

'Religion now', says Seán, 'is getting a terrible battering, but
it'll come back.'

Mary and Seán offer to drive me back to Cork. Seán knows
exactly how long it takes to get to the Shanakiel area, because
he used to have to visit his medical specialist there. 'Exactly
seventeen minutes,' he says. 'Door to door.'

Both Seán and Mary paid to walk through the Jack Lynch
tunnel, on the special day when it was open to pedestrians. 'It
was for charity,' says Mary. 'Sure when would we get the
chance to do it again? It's only for cars.'

As we sweep over the new road in their new, modest, spotless car we can see smoke rising from the bonfires in Togher.

*

Jimmy Murray is a small man who has a high voice. He is from
Ringsend. Jimmy takes off his shoes when he's thinking. 'You
don't mind, do you? I love it. I just do love it.'

Here is Jimmy Murray's plan for the future. He wants to
take the wrecks of old boats, and of old cars, and sink them in
Dublin Bay to make reefs. The objective is to start territorial
fish farming. Jimmy Murray knows that this would work. It
would replenish fish stocks within a ten-mile radius. It would
mean that children could go out fishing with their fathers in

Dublin Bay and not come home disappointed. The reefs would be flood-lit at night, for divers. They would be working models for marine biologists, because, he explains, 'if I'm a fish and I get fed every day I'm going to stay put'.

Jimmy thought all this up in his head, and then discovered, on the Internet, 'An American army guy who dumped tanks into the sea to do the same thing. There's a guy in Japan who makes reefs out of tyres.'

Ideas crowd round Jimmy Murray. 'They're all in my head since a child. It's ongoing, it's frightening. I do try to get away from it.'

*

At nine o'clock on a Saturday morning all you're going to get is people with children; they have to be up at that hour. The Minister is due at nine. He has children. It is midsummer's day, and St John's Day. 'I don't know what they're doing to this world, girl,' says the taxi driver. 'But last night is the worst bonfire night I can remember.' St John's Eve and St John's Day are celebrated in Cork city. There were warnings on the radio yesterday about not using tyres, or other pollutants, to build your bonfires.

At the Cork Women's Poetry Circle in Tig Filí – 'just under the Zanussi sign', they had said on the phone – a long-haired man is dragging a public-address system from a van. Inside there are large bunches of fennel and ivy on the floor, but the

St John's Wort is hard to identify. Someone pointed at a frond of fennel when I asked which was the St John's Wort. This happened several times in the course of the morning. 'A lot of it is not in bloom,' says a woman who is gathering up big bunches of greenery. Someone is opening a fiddle case. One wall of the room is hung with children's drawings to which are attached strongly interpretive labels.

'Herbs for a healthy heart,' says the label on a red squiggle in an abstract sea. 'Blueprint for health,' says the label attached to a toddler's palm prints made in blue paint. Eoghan Clarke, aged five, has drawn a shark. 'Sick hammer shark drawing,' reads the label. 'Eoghan thinks the shark should go to the homeopath just like he does.'

The adults here are mostly in their thirties, and calm-looking, although we are now almost half an hour behind schedule. Even the children are well-behaved. The band in the corner starts to play traditional music.

Breda Dooley is in her early thirties, with long dark hair. She is wearing high heels, quite a short skirt under a man's jacket, and red lipstick. Breda praises the children's paintings later on, in her speech. 'That sort of naïvety is what we need,' she says. 'A clear pure line.'

Today the new office of Consumers for Health Choice Ireland is to be officially declared open. The co-ordinator of CFHCI is Breda Dooley, who went to sit in Micheál Martin's office so soon after he was appointed. The man opening the office is Micheál Martin, who still isn't here, and perhaps that's just as well. By the time ivy has been arranged to tumble over the gallery, by the time one long stalk of fennel has been placed in a green watering can near the exhibition of photographs by Georgia O'Keeffe at the entrance to the Cork Women's Poetry Circle, everyone is a bit puffed.

Micheál Martin arrives looking like a slim and surprisingly young member of the Garda Siochána. He is very tall, and you can see him take a quick breath of dread before entering the room. 'I am very health-conscious,' he says later. 'Some people call me a hypochondriac.'

Breda was thinking on her way in today, in her car, she says, about what she would say in her speech introducing the Minister. But then she decided that 'a lot of what I would say comes from the heart and from passion'.

Micheál Martin looks about him in a familiar but reserved way, like a child prodigy who has been on the concert circuit for a long time, and is beginning to have doubts.

Micheál Martin has a fruit breakfast every morning. He doesn't smoke and he eats lots of salads. He's never used any herbal remedies, except tea tree oil. He won't say what he used tea tree oil for: 'That's a bit personal.' Tea tree oil is very good for treating mouth complaints, says Breda Dooley helpfully. 'Yeah, those little mouth blisters,' says Micheál Martin quickly. He is wearing a sharp suit and a good blue shirt.

'We need, more than ever, herbs from Mother Nature,' Breda is saying. No one is here to oust conventional medicine, she says. She lived in Germany for eight years, and when her little girl was sick she and her husband were very glad of conventional medicine. When her daughter was convalescing the doctors in Germany recommended herbal remedies for her daughter in order to regenerate her body, to regenerate her mind, to regenerate her soul.

'The St John's Wort flower has not opened today and I think that's highly significant. It's looking for change.'

The audience sits quietly through all this; clean-cut, clear-eyed, rational. The sort of audience that a political party can't afford to lose. 'I'm a little bit nervous,' says Breda. 'My mouth is a bit dry, but you know that doesn't matter.' She calls for an integrative health-care programme and the reinstatement of St John's Wort. She says that complementary medicine can free up hospital beds. Then she introduces the Minister, who talks in Irish for almost exactly thirty seconds.

He says in English that it's good to see his Oireachtas colleagues here today: Dan Wallace, TD, Deirdre Clune, TD, and councillor Dan Boyle. Dan Wallace and Dan Boyle are two of the five men present wearing suits. Three of the men present ·have pony tails, and of the three men with pony tails two have cameras.

The Minister explains that the public representatives all have clinics to go to. At meetings with Breda and her team, he says, it emerged that all parties 'want regulation of some sort. It's in the interests of the industry, if I can put it that way. Of the sector.' He manages to say nothing controversial for four or five minutes.

Maureen Morten of CFHCI says: 'Now I invite the Minister to climb the spiral staircase to heaven and open our new office, and then to come back down to Mother Earth and open our "A Picture of Health" exhibition.' I forgot to look at Micheál Martin during this bit.

Upstairs on the gallery the Minister and Breda march past the Eavan Boland room, past the Máire Mhac an tSaoi room and the Eiléan Ní Chuilleanain room, until they come to the door of the new CFHCI office. Breda hands the Minister a pair of garden shears with which to cut the strand of ivy which has been hastily placed at the entrance to the new office door. A newspaper photographer skilfully dodges a child. The Minister and Breda pose for him.

Afterwards the Minister presents the prizes for the paintings in the exhibition. It was not a competition, says Breda: 'There's enough competition in life.' Every child is to have a prize. The Minister is very good at this, except when he says 'Well done, Brendan,' to a child whose name is Daniel. Daniel's mother is stony-faced. Afterwards she and some other mothers complain to Breda that not all the children received prizes, or even had their pictures displayed. A little girl of about seven is sobbing against a man's waist in a self-conscious manner. Breda goes up to apologize to her, but the little girl turns her head away. She is giving it ninety.

'I love the sound of screaming children when they're not your own,' says Elaine, who serves at the coffee bar. Elaine would not call herself a health person. 'No. I smoke. I drink and I have sex on a regular basis.'

An older woman is gathering up all the fresh herbs and putting them into black plastic sacks. Was she going to recycle them, I wondered. 'I'm going to make a great big bonfire,' she said.

*

Mineral water became very fashionable in Ireland about twenty or thirty years after the Famine. That was the time when the technology for aerating water, first used for that commercial purpose by Jacob Schweppe in Switzerland in the eighteenth century, became widely available. The new railways could bring the carbon dioxide canisters across the country. Until 1914 up to 25 per cent of soft-drink sales were mineral water. After the First World War mineral water was re-named soda water, for old officers to splash in their whiskey, and that market was much smaller. At that time the Nash family firm in Newcastle West, County Limerick, was using water from its own well to make lemonade. The quality of the water was crucial to lemonade production up to forty years ago, because the essence of lemon oils used to flavour the drink were very delicate, and disguised nothing.

Richard Nash is a lemonade man, although when we meet in the Shelbourne Hotel in Dublin we are drinking tea. Richard is wearing a pale yellow shirt. He has clear eyes and very good skin. He is in his fifties. He can tell you that lemonade was traditionally white in West Cork and red nearer Limerick. He can tell you about lemonade now: 'Amazingly, lemonade is making a comeback. I was on a radio programme in London called "The Asian Trader", and all they wanted to know about was red lemonade. A lot of them must have had shops in Irish areas. I think the radio station might have been owned by President Assad's brother.'

But Richard is also a water man. He thinks that all our water should be taken from aquifers, which are situated underground. 'It would be cheaper and cleaner. Rivers are literally open sewers.' He knows that the American Bottled Water Association has worked out that only 3 per cent of the public water supply in America is actually consumed. Which raises the question, according to the American Bottled Water Association, of whether it is worth all the expense of making the public water supply potable. Richard Nash knows these things.

In 1979 Perrier launched its mineral water in the United States. Perrier felt the world was waiting for sparkling water, and what sparkling water needed was a mystique, a story surrounding it. In other words, tough marketing. After all, the Americans had developed a bottled water market themselves in places like California and Louisiana where the public water supply was of poor quality. But Perrier was aiming at the urban market on both American coasts.

Richard Nash was watching this carefully.

The family business run by Richard's ancestors was known as Nash's Mineral Waters. In the Seventies it sold water to

Swissair for the annual hajj from Nigeria to Mecca. Richard felt that there was a market in modern Ireland for sparkling water. At the time – although Richard doesn't says this – the culture of success was seeping across the Irish Sea. In London ambitious men had given up drinking alcohol at lunchtime. In November 1983, with his new partner, Geoff Read, Richard launched Ballygowan still mineral water. 'It got nowhere,' perhaps because it was just like tap water, which we were damned if we were going to pay for.

Four months after the launch of still Ballygowan water it was followed by the sparkling version, which took off like a rocket. Sparkling was outselling still water at the rate of four to one. Within two to three years that changed. Now, aside from the pub trade, still water outsells sparkling at the rate of five to one.

In the early Eighties, Richard thinks, 'People felt awkward calling for a Perrier in a pub ... it was seen as a bit pretentious. Ballygowan became stylish in the Irish context, not effete or snobbish.' Perrier must have sold well in the Shelbourne. In Ireland Ballygowan was selling twice as much water as Perrier. It was the other Irish success story, after Bailey's Irish Cream. In the Eighties, when everyone you knew was working in London, Bailey's and Ballygowan were all we had. They were either flashes in the pan or wonderful omens. 'It was greatly over-hyped,' says Richard.

Nevertheless he was confident that Ballygowan could take on Perrier in the States. Perrier, he felt, was not even a high-class product. 'We had a very good strategy. It wasn't as if it was Pellegrino or anything.'

When Perrier had its health scare – the water in some bottles was found to be contaminated – every water company in the world piled into America, and Ballygowan lost its chance to ambush Perrier.

Ballygowan got ready to sell 51 per cent of its share to Anheuser-Busch, who were very eager to get into the mineral water market. But the takeover ended in court. Eventually Cantrell & Cochrane bought Ballygowan. Geoff Read now lives in London and sells quarter bottles of wine to the Irish market and to airlines. After two years Richard Nash re-entered the water market, with a navy blue bottle that looks stylish on restaurant tables.

Last year the water market in Ireland grew by 30 per cent. 'I would guess Ballygowan shift fifty million litres, primarily in big bottles.' Coca-Cola has said that mineral water is the company's third priority after Coca-Cola and Sprite.

Richard is still a water man. He drinks two litres a day, four small bottles. He knows that the public supply is usually chlorinated at night, because the chlorine needs time in contact with the water before it becomes effective. So the chlorine slowly accumulates overnight.

In the morning Richard will only drink boiled water from the public supply. Or he will leave a wide-necked jug of water in the fridge overnight, so that the chlorine can evaporate.

*

In the summer of 1997 one third of Poland was flooded by torrential rain.

'It was three days happening, as I remember,' says Krzysztof Zurek. 'It made people think about what is most important. They work for material things, and all is gone in a split of a second.'

When Krzysztof came to Ireland in 1996 he was shocked by how many people were sick. 'Everywhere you go, cancer, cancer, cancer, by-pass, heart attack.' He is thirty, with a tanned face and red cheeks. He has beautiful teeth. He trained as a holistic massage therapist.

In Poland, says Krzysztof, there are definite seasons. Definite snow, definite summers, definite autumns 'with colours for painters'. The two of us look out at a grey Sligo afternoon, so grey in July that Krzysztof has the light on in his living room, and the only sound is the purr of briquettes in the grate.

It was love that brought Krzysztof here, to the most fluoridated country in Europe. Three per cent of Spain's water is fluoridated – 'just a drop in the ocean', says Krzysztof. Ten per cent of Britain's water is fluoridated, and there have been strong objections to extending fluoridation any further. Seventy-three per cent of the Republic of Ireland's water supply is fluoridated, and there are plans to increase this.

In the bathroom there is square soap in a sea shell and a white nightie drying on the shower stall. Krzyzstof's partner,

Karen Stewart, has taken their baby son, Mikolaj, out with her for the afternoon. 'To respect the subject,' says Krzysztof. I miss them.

The water supply in Sligo has never been better. There was poor supply here throughout the Seventies, Eighties and Nineties. Interrupted supply, water you had to boil, water that was pumped from Lough Gill and periodically polluted.

People used well-water, often bad well-water, as a back-up. Although the population of Sligo town has only gone up by one thousand since 1970, to 18,000 in 1999, thousands of houses have been built in suburban developments. The poor water supply was inhibiting growth. Now there is a new water-treatment plant up at the Foxes' Den in the Tonaphubble townland. It cost four and half million pounds, and although the water is still pumped from Lough Gill, new equipment has changed everything. The new supply 'is better than the water you buy in the shops,' says Jim McGarry, who is a Fine Gael councillor. Unfortunately, one third of Sligo's population is still not connected to the new supply.

Krzysztof had never been part of a political demonstration until he came to live in Sligo. Then he marched through the town to Markievicz House, the local offices of the North-Western Health Board. 'I was very embarrassed,' he says. 'At the same time I want to have good water quality back.'

Markievicz House is named after Constance Gore-Booth, who lived in Lissadell, just outside Sligo town. She married Casimir Markievicz, a Polish count, whom she doesn't seem to have liked much, and adopted Irish nationalism, which she liked a lot.

Krzysztof ended up addressing several public meetings in the Silver Swan Hotel, the Saint Michael Family Life Centre and the Yeats Memorial Building. They were small campaign meetings, attended by maybe sixty people.

Once Krzysztof and Karen started investigating water fluoridation they couldn't believe how little people knew. 'The councillors we talked to know nothing,' he says. 'They even didn't know that Northern Ireland stopped fluoridation in 1997. That never filtered down.' I didn't know that, I say. 'Twenty-five out of twenty-six local councils voted to stop it,' Krzysztof says wearily. 'Same piece of land, same island, our neighbours, and nobody knew.' Krzysztof's co-speaker at the public meetings in the Silver Swan and the St Michael's Family Life Centre was Walter Graham, of the Northern Ireland anti-fluoridation campaign. Two foreigners.

Krzysztof also addressed the monthly meeting of Sligo Council about water fluoridation. Before the meeting he had visited eleven of the councillors personally, in their homes. On 6 March 2000 the council voted unanimously in favour of an anti-fluoridation motion, and sent a letter to the Minister of Health urging him to amend the Health Act of 1960. 'Unanimous,' says Krzysztof. 'That doesn't happen very often. They hardly agree on anything.'

'It's not an issue with people,' says Jim McGarry. 'You won't gain or lose votes with it, although I am very concerned.' The council later reiterated its opposition to the addition of fluoride to mains water at its May meeting.

Krzysztof has photocopies, Krzysztof has newspaper clippings, Krzysztof has books on fluoridation. *Fluoridation: Poison on Tap. Fluoridation: The Aging Factor: How To Recognize and Avoid the Devastating Effects of Fluoride. Fluoridation: The Great Dilemma*, by George Waldbott, MD. Articles on how fluoridated water can thin your bones, make the enamel on your teeth porous (this is called dental fluorosis); articles on how fluoride is more poisonous than lead, how it may be connected to osteosarcoma in young men, on how it builds up in your body, on how hip fractures in older women are higher in fluoridated areas. Studies on how dental decay – fluoride was originally added to the water supply to prevent dental decay in young children – is not significantly lower in fluoridated areas than it is in non-fluoridated ones. This is measured on what is called the DMFT index, which stands for Decayed, Missing and Filled Teeth, and applies to permanent teeth. A study in 1995 in New York State compared the teeth of children in fluoridated Newburgh with the teeth of children in unfluoridated Kingston. The teeth in Kingston were better, although dental fluoridosis was about twice as high in Newburgh. Besides constantly telling you that fluoride is more poisonous than lead, anti-fluoridation campaigners also repeatedly tell you that the improvement in children's teeth in America and Europe since the last world war has everything to do with improved nutrition and dental hygiene, and nothing at all to do with fluoride.

Krzysztof takes papers from his black nylon bag, which is amazingly tidy. 'Oh, I should be born in this country,' he says as he spells out Tonaphubble. 'This information burns,' he says. 'You can't sit on it.' The worst part is that I believe everything he says.

When water fluoridation was first introduced, says Krzysztof, people weren't getting fluoride from other sources, like toothpaste.

He hands me a carton which once contained a tube of Crest toothpaste; he sends me home with a photocopy of the back of the carton. It says: 'Children under 6 yrs: To minimize swallowing use a pea-sized amount and supervise brushing until good habits are established ... Keep out of reach of children under 6 years of age. If you accidentally swallow more than used for brushing, seek professional help or contact a poison control center immediately.'

The fluoride in toothpastes is sodium fluoride, and it is present in a much higher concentration than the hydrofluorosilisic acid which is used to fluoridate drinking water: 0.15 per cent sodium fluoride in toothpaste; 1 part per million of hydrofluorosilisic acid in water.

We are drinking blackcurrant tea, and well water with lemon juice in it. Every week Krzysztof carries about ten five-litre canisters to his neighbour's well, and brings back water for the house.

Fluoride arrives in Ireland from fertilizer manufacturers in Holland, a country that changed its mind about fluoridating its own water in 1976. It is taken by lorry to water boards around the country. The Eastern Health Board is in charge of its distribution.

Krzysztof called the situation in Sligo to the attention of Paul Connett, Professor of Chemistry at Lawrence University in New York state. Professor Connett, who with his wife edits a journal called *Waste Not*, was in Ireland anyway, to speak to groups who were objecting to the construction of incinerators for the burning of rubbish. He told Krzysztof he could devote one day to fluoridation in Sligo. Professor Connett ended up speaking on his own in the Yeats Memorial Building that night. The representatives of the North-Western Health Board, the Department of Health and the Department of Dentistry at University College Cork couldn't make it, and didn't send substitutes.

It would be so simple to stop fluoridation, says Krzysztof. 'No one would lose his job.' I want to run out into the rain and shout, 'Why don't we do that right now?' After your country's blood bank has infected women with Hepatitis C, and haemophiliacs with the AIDS virus, you get a bit jumpy.

'We really need an independent enquiry, like Flood Tribunal, for example,' says Krzysztof. 'Because there is somebody who allows this to happen.' And I wonder if that is true.

*

Everything in the bathroom is getting smaller, to fit into new houses and apartments. Old baths were 800 millimetres in width; new baths are only 700 millimetres. That's four inches narrower.

Michael Colgan of Shires Ireland has a plastic bath at home, and doesn't mind saying so. Michael has seen his market increase by 20 per cent in the last four years. His plastic bath was there when he moved into his house and he never changed it. Bath people don't say plastic, they say acrylic.

A roll-top dual double-sided cast-iron slipper bath, 'like the one in the Flake ad', says Michael, 'would cost the guts of £1,000'. He has sold 14,000 lavatories (the trade calls them pans) in ten months. White is the most popular colour.

*

A baby swims in something like tears. Like tears, amniotic fluid is a cellular free plasma exudate. You could say that amniotic fluid is like blood minus all the cells, as if blood had been put through a sieve. In the early part of the pregnancy the amniotic fluid is richer and yellower. It is a filtration of the mother's blood, and the cells that come off the baby will be suspended in the licor. Around fifteen or sixteen weeks into the pregnancy the baby's kidney system kicks in. He's swallowing the water at one end and pissing it out the other. And so the amniotic fluid becomes more diluted and paler, like your pee after drinking ten pints of water.

It used to be the case that women from the Republic of Ireland travelled to Belfast in order to obtain amniocentesis, which was not available in the Republic because it raised the spectre of abortion. According to one Northern doctor specializing in pre-natal medicine, many still do. 'There would be a couple at each of our clinics,' he says.

Dr Carol Barry-Kinsella works in Dublin, at the Rotunda hospital. She is tall and fair and looks like a bird. She is wearing flat black lace-up shoes which look suspiciously like Doc Martens. Her beeper goes off a lot.

She runs a public clinic, and her patients are well informed. 'They have a very good handle on this before they get here,' says Dr Barry-Kinsella. A large percentage of the women she sees are self-referred. Others are sent by their GPs, or by genetic and paediatric departments who are concerned that the woman has an increased chance of having a disastrously abnormal child, often because she has had one already.

What the woman chooses to do with the information that amniocentesis gives her is her affair. Nobody wants to know what happens next. It could be Mothercare. It could be the airport. Everyone says nothing.

Amniocentesis can't tell you the answers to questions you don't pose. Amniocentesis cannot provide a rubber stamp of normality. That's a common misconception, says Dr Barry-Kinsella. We all carry genetic mutations, 'and that's okay as long as you don't want to have a baby with someone who has the same genetic mutations as you'. There are thousands of genetic disorders and you can't ask questions about all of them.

Surely you can have all the tests if you have the money, I say. Surely someone like Kim Basinger, who had her first child in her mid-forties, would have had herself and her husband Alec Baldwin genetically screened before she conceived?

It's not that unusual for a woman to have a first baby in her mid-forties, says Dr Barry-Kinsella briskly. Neither of us mentions Cherie Blair; Cherie wasn't pregnant when we met. Later Tony Blair would laugh in derision when asked if Cherie would have any pre-natal testing. She is an English Catholic.

A baby's forty-six chromosomes, which contain the genes, 'are forty-six suitcases of information'. Looking for a genetic abnormality, it is as if 'you have to open each suitcase, looking for one red sock'.

It wouldn't make evolutionary sense for abnormal babies to be more likely than normal ones. Even a fifty-year-old woman, at the highest risk of delivering a Down's syndrome child, only has a one in six chance of doing so.

The pregnant women who come to Dr Barry-Kinsella are in a risk group for something: cystic fibrosis, or neural cell abnormality which can lead to spina bifida, or poor cell maturity, or Down's syndrome.

Amniocentesis is invasive. When it is performed, 'the babies come up to have a look at the needle and then move away again', says Dr Barry-Kinsella, though later she says that this description of hers is 'rather fanciful'. I had liked it. Performing amniocentesis at eleven to thirteen weeks was once found to increase the incidence of club foot. I have a friend who was going to be an older mother and whose baby spontaneously aborted after she had amniocentesis. He was perfectly formed. But that was six years ago. With the arrival of real-time ultrasound, so that you can see where the baby is, amniocentesis has become much safer.

Ellen talks fast and moves slow. She is a lawyer, expensively dressed and full of fight. She sits on a board of directors of a company which is composed of eighteen men and one other woman. When she became pregnant – 'I was monstrous from the beginning, I was like Cherie Blair' – her chairman said to her that she was getting fierce stout. After the birth she had to bring a cushion to board meetings.

Ellen had a blood test and a neuchal scan when she was expecting her daughter. The neuchal scan measures the fat pad at the base of the neck of the foetus. In a Down's syndrome child, this neuchal fat pad is very thick. When she was ten and a half weeks pregnant she got on a plane to London. 'I didn't mind the plane. There was something comforting about being somewhere where they had their own sick bags.'

She was thirty-nine years old and pregnant for the first time. She and her partner had decided that she would stop taking the pill to see how they got on. If nothing happened, they were sure they would not be disappointed. Instead, she was pregnant within weeks.

Ellen had read about the neuchal test in a magazine about motherhood. 'My GP had never heard of it. He asked me for a photocopy of the article. I've given it to loads of people since.'

She found the Fetal [*sic*] Medicine Clinic in London to be very different from the private consulting rooms of her obstetrician in Dublin. 'It was all white marble and tinkling fountains and clean magazines. There were loads of women in Laura Ashley cardigans with ribbons on them – they were the staff.'

She had a blood sample taken, and a scan. 'They told me the baby would be born on the 31st of December, and I had it at four in the morning of the first of January.'

After the scan Ellen was told that she had a one in 375 chance of having a disabled child. When the results of the blood test came through three days later she was told that she had a one in 780 chance of having a disabled child. 'We thought we'd done our bit then, and that it would probably be okay.'

Her husband had encouraged her to go for pre-natal testing, and she was glad to go, 'although I was a bit tense because I couldn't smoke'.

If her chances of having an abnormal baby had been high she would certainly have considered abortion. 'It wouldn't have been a moral decision, it would have been a variety of decisions. We're old to be parents and we would have had to think about what would happen to a disabled child when we died. I think the mothers of disabled children are horribly patronized. Everyone says they're great and nobody helps them.'

In the Dublin maternity hospital she attended, Ellen found

people reluctant to talk about pre-natal testing before twelve weeks. 'When I made my first visit to my obstetrician at eighteen weeks, I mentioned that I'd had the tests in England. He said absolutely nothing. Later he returned to the subject. He said, "You know, you could have gone to Belfast …" He didn't actually say what happened there, and I've no idea what does happen there to this day. In the hospital the older men are liberal, the younger doctors are more conservative. I think everyone's nervous of the nurses and what they might say.'

Despite being a privileged private patient – she had the VIP suite when she was having the baby ('Let me tell you, you still have to limp down the corridor, and pass the reception desk, bleeding, to go to the bathroom, and I had half my office in to visit me') – Ellen was unimpressed with how she was treated when she was pregnant. 'All those old magazines. There was nothing like *The Economist*. Nothing to engage your brain. It was all domesticity. And there wasn't even a water cooler for the women waiting there.'

In the end she had a high forceps delivery. She was surprised by how physically tough this was on her obstetrician; she could see sweat running down his nose. Her daughter is fascinated with the question of how she was born, but Ellen doesn't feel she is quite ready for the truth about it, 'so now I have to make crap up'.

She didn't complain because both she and her baby 'got out of it alive'. However, Ellen was in serious pain after the birth. She could not walk easily. 'They give you Voltrol, which is an anti-inflammatory, up your bum. Then afterwards my GP gave me Voltrol Retard, which kills your stomach.'

At her six-week check-up, after the birth, Ellen felt her obstetrician wasn't that interested in her condition. 'Maybe he was worried about litigation. He never referred me to a physiotherapist.'

For three years she was fobbed off by bewildered doctors. In the end, having seized up during a water aerobics class that she thought might help her, Ellen was sent to a physiotherapist and found to have a displaced pelvis, a traumatized sacroiliac joint, and other injuries that were likely to have been sustained by her struggling along despite her condition.

The district nurse in Ellen's town, who is very overworked, told her that she wouldn't visit her because she knew Ellen came from a medical family.

Pregnancy softens the mother's bones. The physiotherapist told her that her injuries were very common, and that if she had been seen within six months of the birth she would have been easy to treat. As it is, Ellen faces two years of physiotherapy, and has a one in two chance of developing rheumatoid arthritis. 'I'll just keep going,' she says. But if Ellen won the lottery, she says, she would set up a trust to improve the way pregnant women are treated. Even if it was just an improvement in the way snippy secretaries treat them; even if it was just providing obstetricians' consulting rooms with sick bags, so that you didn't have to bring your own plastic bag with you; even if it was just having current magazines in the waiting rooms. 'I'd just love to do that,' she says.

*

There is a statue to Sir John Gray on O'Connell Street in Dublin. At the time of Gray's death, in Bath, in 1875, William Wilde commented: 'His monument is in every garret and lane of Dublin.' Now the only people who know who John Gray was are St Louis girls. Their school is in John Gray's old townhouse in Rathmines.

John Gray and William Wilde lived at a time when the professional middle classes – or some of the professional middle classes, anyway – were prepared to plan for the benefit of other people; and the Victorians planned big. It was John Gray who brought pure water to Dublin. Gray was from Mayo, and studied medicine at Trinity College. He was a Protestant who became part of Daniel O'Connell's Repeal movement. He refused the mayoralty of Dublin several times. In 1859, as chairman of Dublin Corporation's Waterworks Committee, Gray demanded an investigation into the city's water supplies. He campaigned, against the bitter opposition of the canal companies, who at that time had a monopoly on supplying water to Dublin, for the passing of the 1861 Waterworks Act. This gave rise to the Vartry scheme, which brought treated water to Dublin through two cast-iron pipes twenty-eight kilometres in length.

The last major addition to the Dublin water system was the building of the Leixlip reservoir in 1966. Then everything went quiet for thirty years. Dublin started losing up to 40 per cent of its water through leaking nineteenth-century pipes. One of the biggest obstacles to zoning more land for the building of new houses is the lack of water supply and of drainage for waste water in the outlying areas of the city. Over the next three years the Department of the Environment and Local Government plans to spend £3 billion on water and waste-water services. There is a water plan in place for 2016. 'Gray took the major leap,' says a city engineer. 'He had vision. We need vision for the long term. We need to think about the next major leap now.'

*

Deirdre is thirty-eight years old, heavily pregnant, and has just come back from a business conference in Madrid. She is a product manager with an Irish branch of a multi-national company. 'If you say "Count me out"' – Deirdre puts her hand up like a schoolgirl – 'Then you're not progressing your career, they think you're not giving the company 100 per cent commitment. They're all so busy watching each other and marking each other.' She loves her job.

Within days of her return home Deirdre passed the airline limit for carrying pregnant passengers, which is set eight weeks from the woman's due date.

'After that they won't insure you,' she says. Deirdre never took more than the statutory fourteen weeks' maternity leave with her previous two babies. She feels her boss would frown on it. 'He has a wife at home who minds and packs his bag for him.'

Deirdre has a little girl and a little boy. Her husband Denis is frequently working abroad – last year for up to six weeks at a time. Denis is a partner in a new business. 'The nature of Denis's start-up is one of the reasons I'm in the day job.' She knows several women who are married to men who have started their own businesses and are working full-time to provide some kind of security and cash flow.

When I rang her to say I wanted to talk to her about how it feels to be a working mother, Deirdre had said: 'Half mad.'

Her greatest advantage, she feels, is that her office is very close to her home.

'It means I can shop in my lunch hour, if I have to. Or I phone the childminder at the end of the day and tell her to have them ready to be thrown into the back of the car when I get home, and be taken to the supermarket. Or occasionally Den does it.'

Every morning she drops Aisling to school at ten to nine. If there is an emergency, like the time Aisling had to have stitches in her head, Deirdre can be there in ten minutes. Her son Tom has a child-minder and she arranges play dates for him. 'I've been so lucky. There's run of four mothers who bring Aisling to ballet. One mother who has a good job in banking changes her working day from eight till two one day a week, and takes them swimming after school, and is delighted to do it.

'If it's pissing my mother picks Aisling up from school automatically. I don't even have to pick up the phone. At the school gates it's a mix, actually. Fifty-fifty, mothers and minders. The minders have their own network.'

Deirdre's current childminder, Bernadette, is thirty-three, a little bit older than the other minders. Bernadette is also pregnant. In two and a half years Bernadette has taken one extra day off, for a funeral. Deirdre got her through an agency. 'You pay through the nose.' Deirdre's old minder, Karen, left because she wanted to gain a childcare qualification, but still babysits for Deirdre. For example, the weekend of the conference from which Deirdre has just returned, Karen came in on Saturday and Bernadette on Sunday. Deirdre pays Bernadette's social insurance stamp; she is an official employee.

'My boss says, "You're fucking crazy. You're ruining her for everyone else."'

*

Catherine McDermott had two girls. With girls you need a lot of water. Catherine McDermott came to her husband's farm near Carrick-on-Shannon when she married, forty years ago. Three generations of McDermotts had lived there before her, and at the time of her arrival the farm's water was taken from the river – since boarded over to protect Catherine's grandchildren – which ran quite close to the house, behind the cattle byres. Water also came from a well on the farm. Catherine and her new husband bored another well, at a depth of forty or fifty feet. 'At that time people put barrels and tanks on the land [to catch rainwater]. There isn't a trace of that now,' she says.

Catherine's favourite colour seems to be green. She is wearing a green cardigan with brass buttons and green trousers. The seven cushions behind me on her sofa are green. Catherine turned the farmhouse into a guesthouse. She has five bedrooms, and two are *en suite*. She's a slim smart woman, who was in hospital a couple of months ago. 'I lost a lot of French in April because of it.'

I too am wearing green – combat trousers – and, I see now, blue socks. A bottle of tonic water exploded over me in the car on the drive down; Catherine says that it's hard to remember to pull over. I eat all the fruit cake she puts in front of me, and share the chocolate biscuits with Catherine's granddaughter, Hazel, who is almost five.

Catherine always thought, and still thinks, that 'a woman is entitled to water in the house. Piped water took a lot of hardship out of life for rural women. I've always said that the house is more important than the cattle.'

Later on she had her daughters. 'And when you have girls you have an awful consumption of water.'

In the early days of her marriage every house in her new area – which lies between Elphin and Carrick-on-Shannon, and measures about twenty-two square miles – had a well. 'They're all boarded up now,' she says. The farmers drove their cattle to rivers to drink. On the farm she grew up on, in Carrick-on-Shannon, there had been no piped water either, until about 1958 or 1959 when her family fitted a tank under the house which recycled water for household use.

Then the farmers' herds got bigger, as they went into dairying. 'I heard the men talking at a meeting the other night,' she says. 'And they were saying people would have fifty or sixty head of cattle nowadays. There wouldn't have been that amount of cattle here in the past.'

The new milking parlours used a lot of water, as do the modern slatted sheds where cattle are over-wintered from October to April. The sheds have to be washed out. The cattle have to be provided with drinking water for up to seven months of the year. 'Our one big problem is leaking cattle troughs,' she says. 'When the farmers take the cattle in, the troughs out in the fields could be leaking all winter. Everyone's land has to be walked to check up on the troughs.' The group water schemes have the authority to enter farms to check this, and carrying out the checks is hard work. 'People only appreciate the water when it's turned off,' she says.

Catherine's group water scheme started in 1979 when a committee was formed. 'It was four men and myself,' says Catherine, 'and it is still four men and myself. No one wants to get involved.' The group meets here in Catherine's house, and the meetings can go on until one or one-thirty in the morning. 'We enjoy the chat. Mr Carney is eighty.'

Each participant in the new scheme paid £300, and the government funded the balance. Catherine spent a lot of time at the Department of Environment Group Water Scheme section in O'Connell Bridge House in Dublin, sorting out the paperwork. She dealt with the same civil servant every time. 'Mary Doyle was a lovely lady, the loveliest person.'

The group water scheme put a pump house on the shores of Lough Corbally to draw its water. They put in a booster pump to improve pressure. The houses were often considerable distances apart.

There were about 180 households on the scheme in 1979, and almost 200 in 1999. The scheme was never intended to be as big as it is now, and the water pressure is not good. The increase is attributable to the new houses in the area and also the fact that new households have signed on to replace those who left the scheme 'because the water was so bad. It looks brown in a bucket. Every month it is tested and it's not fit for human consumption. There's *e. coli* and everything in it. Then three or four years ago we had the algae bloom, and the council closed the whole water scheme down in July. There was the smell, the whole lot. There's so much fertilizer used in farming these days, and the nitrates could be coming down a drain miles away. Algae blooms in still weather and every day during the summer I look out and hope there's a breeze.'

Catherine would never connect her washing machine or her dishwasher to the lake water. She used piped water from her own well for that. But many of her neighbours had no choice, and connected machines up to the lake water. 'They just cleaned the filters more often,' she says. The water was all right if you boiled it, it was fine for cattle. It is bog water, with a bit of lime in it, and if you store it in a tank it settles and becomes quite clear. Catherine thinks this method is better than chlorinating the water. There has been some talk, in English agricultural magazines, that chlorinated water is bad for cattle.

In 1999 the water scheme turned to a new source of water, the nearby Polecat springs, four miles up the road. It had to exert political pressure on the county council to get a 75 per cent grant to access the springs. 'Now we'll have the best water in County Roscommon,' says Catherine, who is resolutely cheerful.

They laid pipes along the side of the road to get to the springs, which are not far from it. When they had to cross people's land with the pipes people were very good to them, Catherine says. Farmers who weren't on the scheme, and couldn't benefit from its expansion, allowed them to lay pipes on their farms. Two other water schemes, from Aughrim and Creeve, are already using the Polecat springs to supply their water, and all three schemes will amalgamate. The springs are thought to be pretty well inexhaustible. There will be two twenty-horsepower pumps, 'instead of the two three-horsepowers we had for the lake water, running them into the ground'.

There is now a pilot filtration scheme being fitted at no extra cost, organized by the National Federation of Group Water Schemes and Roscommon County Council. 'That's a great boost,' says Catherine. 'It's funded by the government, using European money.'

Now there is nothing else to do on the water scheme, says Catherine, 'other than closing it off and getting a new committee'.

*

S.F. Cody's solitary Irish branch, in Arnott's department store in Dublin, is an homage to the romance of staying in, of getting ready, of being a fulfilled career girl who likes to relax after working at her wonderful job. She has been advised that every day she must make time for herself, to get in touch with her intuitive side, to change how she feels. A bath is much easier than yoga, much simpler than meditation. It is also true that there is nothing like the first bathroom in which you can use as much hot water as you like without being yelled at.

Although there are hints of raciness in S.F. Cody – like the Kama Sutra Botanicals Massage Oil, to give just one example – the ideal S.F. Cody customer seems to be someone who spends a long time in the bathroom, getting ready and dealing with stress. Soaps, bath gel, bath foam, after-bath lotion and anything you care to massage yourself with is stacked on every side.

There are fifteen different varieties of Bath Bomb.

The Bath Bombs come in Cool Jazz, 'to uplift and revitalise you before a WILD night out'; Tutan Kalmer, 'a blend of exotic oils as used by ancient civilisations'; and Totally Wrecked: 'For the ultimate hangover pick-me-up drop this into your bath.

The oils will clear the foggiest head!!'

Bath Bombs are made from sodium bicarbonate, adiphic acid, alic acid, sodium borate, pentasodium, tiphosphate, fragrance and artificial colouring. Loose spa salts are also available, at £5.50 per bag.

S.F. Cody sells a book, *The Art of the Bath*, which costs £15.50. The sentence 'She could not tell where the water stopped and the her body began' is emblazoned on the back cover. If only that had ever been true.

The Art of the Bath gives a guide to nine different fibres and weaves which can be used to make bath towels. It tells you to bathe your baby in camomile flowers.

A young girl holds a tube of Bath Fizz droplets under her mother's nose. 'The strawberry is lovely,' says her mother. The girl moves on quickly. Shopping with your mother is a nightmare. 'Wouldn't it be lovely to have lots of money?' says her mother. The girl does not reply.

4
[moving]

Just imagine that you were going through a bad time, fighting with your partner, and one day you came home to see a removal van parked outside your house. A huge lorry with a tail lift, and two men carrying things into it. Not his furniture (he doesn't have any furniture; he arrived at your door with two plastic bags, an overcoat and a painting of Elvis Presley), but male things nevertheless. A filing cabinet. A masculine lamp.

But not his lamp. The angel of bad relationships has flown up and down your street, and put an invisible mark on your door. You are filled now with the excitement of a narrow escape, the thrill that comes from witnessing a car accident, or attending the premature funeral of an acquaintance. You can feel your eyes shining.

All over the country people can hear their neighbours fighting. Walls are thin. I knew a woman who lay awake at night listening to the man who lived next door beating up the woman who lived with him. 'It was the drugs,' said their neighbour, who is a bit too kind. She dreaded going to bed each night, to hear the beating and the screaming.

People can hear the two of you arguing; when you argue you can be heard in the street. But most houses with a sudden removal van outside their door have been silent for a while. There is silence down the end of the phone as your mother, who was practically born married, listens to you talk about this. 'It's when you stop fighting the troubles start,' she says. 'When you don't even care enough to fight with each other.'

You are stuck behind the net curtains, spying. You don't have to face the neighbours, the bank manager, both families, and any friends the two of you had left. You don't have to put up with kindly enquiries. Men usually move out quickly. It can be anything from a few black sacks in a taxi, to a swift removal van they cannot fill. In any event, the vehicle will be shrouded in self-pity and, frequently, surprise.

*

Carrickmines Wood is a development of sixty houses and seventy-two apartments and penthouses – so far. The sixteen big houses, in the cul de sac on your left as you drive in, were priced at up to £1.2 million each, and all sixteen were sold out within a day. Out of the eight houses that are occupied on the left-hand side of the cul de sac, we count four jeeps, one Jaguar and a Porsche. A few minutes later, when I wind down the window of our own car to ask a woman what section of houses we are in, the window falls straight down into the cavity of the car door. 'That's it, we're going to be arrested,' says my boyfriend. The woman has lovely arms, which must have been earned in a gym. She is placing an abundance of plants – some of them could be hedging – in the earth of her front garden. 'Which houses are these?' I ask. 'The Shaw,' she says, and smiles. She knows it's a silly naming system.

The overwhelming impression at Carrickmines Wood is of the colour yellow. The two completed apartment blocks are yellow. The rocks round the Japanese-style pond at the entrance, in which arum lilies stand in bunches, are yellow. The fine gravel or grit there is yellow. The ESB electricity box is housed behind the pond, not far from the deck, and it has been built into a little dolmen-type shelter made of pale stone.

The £1.2 million houses are red brick and yellowish stucco. They have double garages and pitched rooves. The garages have pitched rooves too; the kind of roof that you could put a clock tower on. Their porches are supported by wooden pillars and their low fences are made up of yellowish stone with stained four-by-fours stretched above. As you look round the whole development from the Japanese-style pond, at the yellow apartments with palms on the top balconies, at the wide roads, you wonder where you are. It could be a holiday village in southern Spain or perhaps Florida, rather than a housing estate in south Dublin.

'People want apartments and townhouses now,' said an

auctioneer. The type of development where you can live like a millionaire and an ordinary person at the same time, where you can look out your window to see the Jaguar and your kids playing with the neighbours' kids. 'With the new density guidelines developers can now cram in smaller houses and apartments and make the same type of money.'

Park Developments, which built Carrickmines Wood, was an old McInerney company. Mr Daniel McInerney, brother of one of the founders of Park Developments, lived on the same road, back down through the crossroads, as Carrickmines Wood. I went carol-singing along here once, when I was about thirteen. Mr McInerney, who as I remember was wearing a blazer, gave a contribution which was enough to satisfy even a gang of picky little girls. We also called to houses round the corner, on Glenamuck Road, and sang to Mick Jones, then the guitarist with the Rolling Stones. He looked terrified of us all. You could see him remembering to do the right thing. They say now that Mick Jones' contribution to the Rolling Stones was greatly underestimated at the time.

Samuel Beckett also lived just a few doors down from Carrickmines Wood, in a mock-Tudor house called Cooldrinagh; doors in Carrickmines are placed fairly far apart, or used to be. On Brighton Road we count intercoms on the gate posts – we stop at fifteen – and applications for planning permission. The Japanese ambassador's residence, in Oakfield, is ringed by steel fencing. 'Sure you wouldn't get it in Mountjoy,' said the security guard.

At the next house, Hollybrook, there is a planning application on a gate pillar announcing the wish to demolish the house and build forty-two apartments on 1.24 hectares. Old houses in Carrickmines are not beautiful, just big. It is the gardens that are beautiful. Beckett's mother May was a keen gardener.

There are seven different types of houses in Carrickmines Wood, and the most expensive type, the £1.2 million type, is called after Beckett, poor bastard. Then there is the Yeats, and the Swift. The Beckett, the Yeats and the Swift are all included in the cul de sac on the left, and vary almost imperceptibly from one another. The Yeats is distinguished by a detached garage. Floor space in this first cul de sac is about 3,600 square feet per house.

The houses that sold for more than £735,000 were the Joyce and the Kavanagh. It was the Shaw which was the cheapest and went for £735,000. The Joyces and the Kavanaghs are interspersed amongst the Shaws. There is no Flann O'Brien house or Behan house, but then the one always went home drunk and the other never went home at all. There is no writer's name assigned to the new townhouses yet.

Amongst the people who bought the £1 million houses in Carrickmines Wood were: Pat Stuart, who sold his stake in a dot.com company for £17 million; Colin Glennon of Glennon Insurances; Richard Murphy, former head of Xtravision; Danny Durkan of the Durkan building family. Young, professional, self-employed. No one says millionaire. 'The sort of people who bring home the £14.99 bottle of wine, not the £4.99 bottle of wine that you and I buy,' said the auctioneer. 'People with kids like the housing estate, because it's safe.' Some of these buyers had returned from England. One couple were home from the U.S. All were, originally, southsiders, and in that way they were local people.

The houses came with wooden floors and big kitchens with stainless-steel cookers. They are surprisingly close together.

*

In Finglas, Gina is saying: 'Let's see now. Young couple there, a single person on her own, a young couple rearing a young family, a man on his own, a widow, a young couple, Eileen Devitt, next door's empty, ourselves, a young couple with no family, a couple in their forties, a young couple who moved in two years ago, a young couple who moved in just recently.'

Gina is naming the residents of her cul de sac, a list she has almost by heart. She's lived in Finglas East for thirty-five years.

Fiona McGowan, the local auctioneer, is saying: 'Finglas East is the oldest part of Finglas, the closest to Glasnevin. Some people call it Glasnevin North. Now the younger couples are moving in. It's one of the few places first-time buyers can afford. White-collar workers are living up and down the Bally-gall Road.'

In St Helena's Resource Centre Joan Duffy is saying: 'Anyone who moves into Finglas has some connection to Finglas. I was reared in Ballygall Crescent. I lived in Berryfield, Finglas South, for twenty-two years. Then we moved to Oakwood, Finglas East again. My daughter wants to move to a settled area. She doesn't like the new estate thing. Two and a half years ago she bought a house in Finglas West for £59,000. She sold it for £100,000. I said to her, "Rebecca, that's just not right."'

Helen Maher is buying the house next door to Gina's. Helen Maher is saying: 'I'm waiting for the auctioneer. Oh, it's a lovely, really cosy house. It has panelled doors, latch-key presses, and floorboards, I'll just be able to sand them. An elderly couple lived here and the wife died in June. The husband has gone to live with the family.'

Frank O'Leary, in *Finglas: A Celebration*, is saying: 'Like the Venice of Ruskin, the Finglas of 100 years ago is now part of a romantic past buried forever in the technology of modernity.'

Fiona McGowan is saying: 'People in Finglas stay with their houses a long time. At least until their mortgages finish.'

Gina is saying: 'Is her name Helen? The name of the old woman who used to live there was Helen as well. Helen and Myles were here when we moved in. They were twenty years older than us. Helen was a great gardener, you can see her glasshouse out the back there. She used to grow tomatoes and cucumbers in it.'

In St Helena's Resource Centre, Margaret Naughton Doyle is saying: 'I'm very defensive about Finglas South.'

In St Helena's Resource Centre, Margaret and Joan's colleague, Lorraine Merriman, is saying: 'I hate it now. The people buying there are all related to bogies [dodgy people]. Finglas South is full of anti-social behaviour. They just left it to brew. They plastered over all the problems. If you're out of their league, say you're a kid with a bit more intelligence, they don't like it and they'll pick on you. I don't blame the police for being afraid they'll get a kicking.'

Fiona McGowan is saying: 'I've worked with Mason Estates for five years. I worked in our Phibsboro office, but there was so much demand here that we had to open a full-time office.'

Margaret Naughton Doyle is saying: 'When my marriage broke up I moved back to my mam's house in Pinewood. Now I wouldn't walk up the road I lived on for twenty years in Finglas South. It's very rough. It's gone.'

Helen Maher is saying: 'I'm a midwife. I'm originally from Thurles. I spent a couple of years in Sydney, Australia, I lived in Cork until April, then I decided to move to Dublin, and I rented a flat in Dublin in July. I'm paying £260 per month, which is the best part of my mortgage now.'

Gina is saying: 'I wasn't a great mixer in those days. I found it hard to make friends. I've got better. I suppose I've matured.'

Lorraine Merriman is saying: 'I moved to Clonee. It's great. You don't hear a sound. It's a different world. There's no one out there who doesn't work. Both sides of me are rented.'

Fiona McGowan is saying: 'With the M50 now nowhere is too far.'

Gina is saying: 'At that time there were only four or five cars in the cul de sac, out of about twenty houses. People went into town very seldom. There was a little shop at the end of McKee road did school uniforms. She still does, as a matter of fact.'

Helen Maher is saying: 'I heard it was built by a co-op, that it's a big C of I area. You can tell by the gardens.'

Gina is saying: 'Helen was C of I, Myles is a Catholic. Three or four doors up, they're C of I as well. The houses were always well looked after, and the new people are just the same and keep it tidy. The gardens sometimes improve when they're sold, because as people got older they weren't able to maintain them. A lot of the front gardens are done away with, with the drive-ins.'

Fiona's colleague Alison is saying: 'I used to be in banking. Now I'm dealing all the time with first-time buyers. We work six days a week. You can only do this job if you really love it.'

I'm saying: 'You get commission, don't you?'

Joan Duffy is saying: 'We have a job-creation programme based around equestrian, media and marketing. It's called Le Ceile, and it's part of the European Network Initiative, Recite II.'

Alison is saying: 'We're an all-female office. So is our Booterstown branch. So is our Ranelagh branch. It's the ladies who are selling the houses. Male auctioneers are intimidating; they're up there with the solicitor and the doctor. People are afraid of them.'

Gina is saying: 'Helen fell and broke her hip. I used to slip in to her every morning. For the first six months after she fell I'd be in to her twice a day. I did her shopping for her. Helen was a very independent person. She appreciated anything you did for her.'

Joan Duffy is saying: 'There are over 200 horses in Finglas. That book *Pony Kids* was a godsend to us. I took it over to Brussels to convince the Italians. Up to then they didn't believe it.'

Alison is saying: 'It's the ladies who are buying the houses too. Sometimes you never meet the husband at all. You say: "Do you want to get him to have a look?" And she says, "No, he says whatever I decide is okay." Most of them are very young, about twenty-odd.'

Gina is saying: 'Myles had had a stroke eight years ago, which affected his memory and his sight. He went into a home when Helen fell, and that was one of her great regrets. Helen missed having him there.'

Joan Duffy is saying: 'That Corpo grant they gave out in the Eighties, for people to move out, did untold damage. It took all the good people out of the area. It was the beginning of the end of what we had. They left for other parts of Finglas, for Crumlin or for Palmerstown.'

Gina is saying: 'I miss Helen. I'd only been in to her the day before. Helen had one of those speed-dial thing where she only had to press a button to make a phone call, and the first button she pressed was mine. I threw on my dressing-gown and went in. She was in a terrible state.'

Margaret Naughton Doyle is saying: 'The Craigie family, which owned the Merville dairy, this used to be their house. Saint Helena's. The Eastern Heath Board took the house over then as a family resource centre. This was the old kitchen. We kept the old Aga. It's not working.'

Joan Duffy is saying: 'We still haven't received one ecu for job creation.'

Gina is saying: 'Only one week later the doorbell went and it was Helen's son and daughter-in-law to say that she had passed away during the night. She was buried from the C of I church in Finglas. Even the priest went. He used to come round with communion for Myles.'

*

Eamonn Finn has a special computer package called Easimove which was invented for removal companies. Eamonn is at his company, Allen Removals, every day from seven until about five-thirty, and on Saturday mornings. 'I don't be tired,' he says. 'The computer system watches everything. It's not hard work now, but it was one time.'

The Easimove system creates a special diary for the estimators – the men who gauge how many square feet your belongings are going to take up in the removal lorry, and the type and number of packing crates that are going to be needed. It automatically sends customers letters confirming the day of the move, and price quotations. It sends mailshots to the person in the house that the Allen Removals customer has bought, looking for their business too. It makes a diary of tomorrow's work, runs the invoice file and the credit limits, and draws up a job sheet.

Eamonn had faxed me a week's job sheet after just one enquiring phone call, and he asked no questions. In fifteen years of journalism in Ireland this is the first time that I can remember anyone voluntarily surrendering a business document, complete with names and addresses and prices charged.

'Eamonn is very straight,' says Pat, who drives one of Allen's thirteen removal trucks. Once Pat ran his lorry into a client's car. The client was a Protestant clergyman, who, to Pat's surprise, shopped around for a cheap quote on the repairs. 'Eamonn said, "You cost me fucking two thousand pounds,"' says Pat, imitating a country accent. 'And he never mentioned it after that.' Pat gets slagged off by his colleagues about his own country accent, about being a culchie. He is from Wicklow town.

Eamonn Finn is from Ballaghadreen in County Roscommon, and his life can be said to have been built around the internal combustion engine; although he doesn't say that. His own family had a haulage firm – 'three or four lorries' – which moved cattle and farm machinery and worked for local quarries. 'There was nothing in Ballaghadreen then.' Eamonn was one of the three boys in his class who didn't emigrate to England or America. 'All the fellas gone. Only girls were left.' Eamonn had a car when he was sixteeen. By the time he left school he was running his own truck. In the winter months, the quiet time in the haulage business, 'I'd go over to London.

All the lads were over there.' He seldom goes back to Bal-laghadreen now. 'My parents are gone.'

Eamonn has a huge double desk, a shiny leather couch with studding, and some nervous-looking potted plants. He puts on his glasses to read small print and his computer screen. He is a stocky man. He drives a Mercedes. Underneath this office lies the warehouse, where acres and acres of timber packing cases, piled to the ceiling, wait for their owners to come home, or find another. The warehouse is a cathedral of waiting, of hundreds of futures on hold.

On his desk is the picture of a dark young man, smiling into the flash. You sense a party going on around the boy, although he takes up the whole photograph. This is Eamonn Finn's elder son, Paul, who died in a car accident. He was twenty-three. 'You never get over it.'

Eamonn started Allen Removals – he chose the name because it was easy to spell and would be first in the phone book – in 1975. Those were the days of wrapping in newspaper and straw – 'newspaper stains everything' – and of the tea chest. Eamonn used to drive himself. He loved being on the road. 'I haven't driven one now in a long time.'

'I used to work for the government. I was a civil servant in the Department of Agriculture, working in meat storage and control. I never liked it. It was a waste of time, a waste of space. You'd be better off staying home and going to the pub. You go into work and achieve nothing. I never really had an interest in it.'

There wasn't much competition in the removal business in the Seventies, and fuel costs were low. He started with two men and his secretary Pauline Rudden, who still works for him. 'When I'm not here Pauline runs things. She knows what it's about.'

There isn't much about the business that Eamonn doesn't like. 'Five to ten years ago a lot of people were losing their houses. You'd be packing children's toys, wedding albums, everything. Women crying in the doorway. If you didn't do it then someone else would, but still you don't like to see the name on your truck outside the house where that's happening.'

The removal business is a masculine world. Removal men, says Eamonn, are individualistic. It's hard work, but they like it. Drivers get a basic wage of £350 per week. Their customers are overwhelmingly women. 'Ninety per cent women, booking and organizing. Most people are very worried about moving. It's a big ordeal to uproot your memories.'

Eamonn has moved house three times. 'The wife done all the packing.'

*

Marie McLoughlin lives in a semi-detched house in Swords and is moving today to a detached house in Drogheda which has an extra bedroom. Marie doesn't know a soul in Drogheda. 'It's daft, really,' she says. Her husband, Keith, is in Kazakhstan. 'I know,' she says. 'It's incredible.' Keith works selling software for telephone systems accounts. The two elder children, Patricia who is ten and David who is seven, are on their last day at their Swords school. Andrew, who is one and a half, is taken away in the middle of the morning to be minded by a neighbour.

Marie had hoped to move on Monday. But the woman who has bought their house wants them out today, because she is going away on Monday. She is a single woman who has bought the house as an investment. She lives in Malahide. Marie knew that Keith would be away in Kazakhstan for a fortnight, he is due home tonight, and she wanted him here for the move. 'This is why,' she says, gesturing to the party balloons, the television still churning out children's programmes even though Andrew has left, and the breakfast bowl half full of cereal.

Everything was going fine until the life insurance company lost the doctor's certificate which confirmed that Keith is in perfect health. The bank won't release the cheque for the new house until it receives the form. Marie won't know if she's getting the key of the Drogheda house until some time this morning.

Kevin is the driver of the Allen Removals lorry that is parked outside Marie's house – 'I'm known for acquiring tips' – and Stephen, Frank and Eoin are working with him today. Kevin strongly advises Marie to get the key before lunchtime, because on Fridays builders are known to like liquid lunches, which can go on until five o'clock. The removal man's contempt for banks, solicitors and builders – in fact anyone who is charge of handing over keys – is bottomless. 'The tension is crazy,' says Marie.

Marie is a very calm woman whom I suspect is a Christian. There is a calendar in the kitchen, looking down on Frank while he wraps delph, and this month's picture shows Christ Healing the Lame, Matthew 11:4–6. Not that this proves anything. It is Marie, with no make-up and an air of cheerful resignation, who is the main clue. Later on, she tells me she worked for Trocaire before she got married. And then she worked for the hospice movement.

The McLoughlins have lived in Swords for seven years. It is a nice quiet cul de sac, and there used to be lots of children. But now the road is 'becoming rental', as Marie puts it. On one side of Marie is a house full of four teenage boys. 'They're fairly noisy,' says Marie. 'It's their nature.'

'All the houses over there,' says Marie, pointing out her front window to the opposite side of the road, 'are four-bedroom. They won't move.'

Some of the houses have been bought privately by double-income families with no children. 'It's the double-income couples who have the money,' says Marie, without resentment.

Three out of the thirty houses on the road are now rented. It's hard to resist the prices offered by investors. When Marie bought this house she paid £49,000 for it. The single woman investor, whom Marie thinks works in the airport, paid £125,000.

While Frank makes tea for us all in the kitchen, Marie talks about Drogheda. 'It's a brand new house, detached – one sugar please. It's nice to have someone else making it. The kids are fine about it. They live in the present. The girls in Patricia's class all signed her t-shirt.'

Moving is so expensive, says Marie, and it's hard to keep track of where all the money is going. She has only moved once before, when Patricia was two and David was a newborn. 'Keith was around then and he's great. It was just a matter of packing things into a van.'

The worst thing Eoin ever found while doing a removal was some 'horribly dirty women's underwear, not too long ago. And a book on Satan-worshipping and religious sex.' Finding sex guides is commonplace, Eoin says. He is nineteen.

People write thank-you letters to removal men. 'They say thanks very much, you made our lives easy,' says Stephen. He is putting Patricia's young clothes into a cardboard wardrobe. The cardboard wardrobes come from Smurfit's.

'We moved Michelle Rocca but she kept to herself. She wouldn't talk to us. She's got a lot on her mind. We moved your woman out of *Father Ted*, who played Sister Assumpta [this is the actress Rose Henderson]. She's a lovely woman and her house was the nicest I've seen so far. Not the biggest, but the nicest. We moved your man out of *Crimeline* in January.' Stephen is twenty-three.

Frank is in Marie's kitchen, wrapping coins. 'She has a fascination with change,' he says.

At 12.07 precisely Frank moves a pile of cardboard crates (Allen Removals get through 1,000 cardboard crates per week) to reveal the dishwasher which had been hidden behind them. The dishwasher is full of clean delph.

'Shit,' says Frank.

At 12.25 he and Kevin plumb out the washing machine, even though, strictly speaking, they're not supposed to do that.

In the housing development in Drogheda the grass on the central green is newly sown. The windows of the houses next to the McLaughlins still have masking tape on them. 'We can't put the beds upstairs,' Eoin tells Frank. 'The smell of varnish would knock a fucking buffalo over. They were still painting the stairs when we went in. It's always the same. It's always the same.'

Marie thinks that the builder only remembered that they were moving in today when she phoned him at lunchtime. The McLoughlins bought this house for £149,000 and the same houses are selling for £170,000 now, so they have done very well.

The lights over the sink still aren't installed, 'although I've been asking and asking'. There's no cooker and no fridge in the kitchen, which has a utility room off it and a view of more semi-detached houses being constructed behind the breeze-block back garden wall. The cooker and the fridge are to be delivered this afternoon.

The hall, stairs and landing have wooden floors, which Kevin reckons have only been sanded and varnished on Monday or Tuesday of that week. He's going to put the beds in the living room, and the McLoughlins are going to have to camp for a couple of days.

Everything smells new. The master bedroom has fitted wardrobes, an en suite bathroom and a view over the green. Marie is phoning about the cooker and the fridge, on her mobile – the phone is not connected yet. 'That's more our fault than theirs,' says Marie. 'I've yet to fill in the form.'

The cab of a removal truck will only hold three adults, but there is a pod above the cab where drivers sleep on overnight jobs. This can take the overflow when things get crowded in the cab.

On the way back to Dublin, Stephen and Eoin, being the youngest, are in the pod. They leave the door to the pod open, and pin up a picture of a blonde with enormous breasts. 'We're mocking you from a height,' Eoin calls down to me.

*

Tom is young and handsome in a suit and when he's relaxing he wears amazingly fashionable backless shoes, with no socks. He is so well dressed that I wonder if he is gay. During the day Tom is part of the flotilla of young men circulating on the pavements of Baggot Street or Fitzwilliam Square in south Dublin, wearing the right sunglasses and talking on very small mobile phones. At night he works on his new house, which cost £242,000, on Dublin's north side. In a bar on Pembroke

Street at lunchtime Tom is unremarkable. We have cappucci-
nos. In the working-class pub near his new home, Tom,
although he is dressed in denim jeans and a t-shirt, like many
of the men there, looks like a creature from another planet. It
might be the backless shoes, it might be the slight tan, but Tom
looks richer than anyone else.

Two years ago Tom was earning £20,000 per year punch-
ing code for an Irish software company that has made its fortune 'providing the building-blocks which allow companies to
do business on the Net'. Now he can't really remember how
much money he has. He's a stock-option millionaire. 'Let me
see. Jesus, I'm frightening myself now. Probably about £1.2
million at the rates four or five weeks ago. It's paper money,
it's free money. It goes up and down. Now it's half that.'

When Tom met his girlfriend he didn't tell her about the
money for the first five months of their relationship. She took
the news calmly. 'It didn't matter to her,' says Tom. He sold
some shares to buy the new house, and took out a £75,000
mortgage.

In the office there is never any talk about money, nor is it
discussed socially. 'That's regarded as sort of uncouth.' But the
real reason that no one talks about their windfall is that no one
knows how many share options their colleagues got. 'If you sit
down with someone and find out that they got a whackload
more than you did, you don't want to generate self-doubts and
fears. The shares were issued in bands and any smart company
will keep the composition of those bands secret.'

So money has swept silently through the company, with colleagues watching each other for signs of change. Three or four people have bought cars. There was talk of someone who bought a second-hand Lexus. There's a Volkswagen Cabriolet in the car park, and another nice Ford. Half a dozen, like Tom, have bought houses.

'I know people in the company who are buying houses for a couple of their friends who would never be able to afford them. I know people who are sending their parents on £5,000 holidays. Or donating shares to charities. Some people feel it's not totally deserved. I haven't deserved all this.'

When Tom took his job there were about sixty people working in the company. He knew everyone who worked there. Now the company employs 750 to 800 people worldwide. 'When I started, in one day you could be marketing, then writing code and writing press releases. You could be doing anything. That's kind of fantastic. It's not sustainable, but it's fantastic.'

The share option has bound Tom more closely to the company – he will only get the full pay-out if he stays three years – although many of his colleagues felt pretty closely bound to it already. They don't take their twenty days holidays per year because there's always something important going on. There is a sense of collective responsibility. It's kind of funny to see senior men, who have no financial reason to work so hard, putting in long hours. 'They like to be pushing forward and getting bigger. Not themselves, the company.'

But Tom doesn't want to keep going much longer. He is thinking of becoming a maths teacher. He has taught before. 'In a group of thirty people, five of them will be bored senseless. Five of them will understand everything, no matter what you do. It's the other twenty I am interested in. To see the understanding on their faces. I love explaining, to put things in an understandable format and see them go, "Jesus, I never thought of that." That's a great feeling.'

*

At the First Steps Montessori school in Ely Place, Dublin, you can watch your child all day, if you want to. You can watch him on a live video link-up. This morning there are nine children present in the younger of the two classes, aged between two and three. They are getting ready for their morning walk. A small camera surveys them from a high window frame.

The camera system cost £1,500, says Andrea McDonnell, who owns the school and is sharply tailored. 'At the end of the day the parents would have paid for it themselves,' she says.

Seven little boys and two little girls are walking calmly to their small seats at small tables, wearing their special Lego navy jackets. The girls wear pretty tartan Sarah Louise skirts and the boys wear ties; they look like miniature bank managers. Andrea's mother wholesales the uniforms.

Prime viewing time comes later this afternoon, at 2.30, when the children's drama class starts. That's when parents will be able to slip a disk into their computers and link up to the First Steps video cameras. Dance class on Tuesday is another big draw, as is the Spanish class. The children obligingly count up to ten in Spanish for an incredulous outsider. 'It's the language of the future,' says their teacher Kay Ryan.

'We have one parent who regularly watches from Scotland or Turkey,' says Andrea. 'The system's also useful if a parent is worried about a child. For example, Conor's father was worried that he wasn't eating. He could tune in at lunchtime. It's a way of getting to see them.' Sometimes parents tune in at the end of the day to see if their child is the last in the school to be collected.

'Mila and Lucca's father is in Yugoslavia quite a bit. During the summer his parents were able to tune in and see their grandchildren for the price of a phone call.'

One mother uses First Steps to mind her child three or four days a week. She leaves her house in Navan at 7 a.m. to get the 7.15 bus, has her son at First Steps for 8.30, and then picks him up at around 5 to get the 5.30 bus, just round the corner from the school. On Fridays Kay Ryan often gives them a lift to the Gresham on O'Connell Street, which is where the bus leaves from on Friday. At the end of the week, Kay is more concerned about the mother than the son. 'Sure he's alright, he sleeps on the bus on the way home' she says.

*

Ten years ago Tom Hyland drove the number 10 bus. A television documentary about him was called 'From the Number Ten to Dili'. His conversation is still punctuated by bus numbers, as in: 'When we first got the typewriter, and it was a golf-ball typewriter, real heavy, we carried it down the bottom of O'Connell Street to get the 78A back to Ballyfermot.' And when he heard that Bishop Belo and the East Timorese foreign minister in exile had won the Nobel Peace Prize between them, 'I danced round the office. Then I locked up the office and went out to get the 22 to tell the lads.'

In Tom Hyland's conversation, the lads are either (a) bus drivers (as in 'I do see the lads driving round town and they always give you the thumbs-up sign'); or (b) East Timorese exiles he has brought to Ireland. 'Portuguese passports, you see.'

Despite a fear of flying, Tom has made several trips to East Timor as head of the Ireland East Timor Solidarity Campaign. He once visited East Timorese exiles in Lisbon, the capital of the old colonial power in East Timor. He found them living in hostels – 'and the hostels weren't great, either'. He told them they had to get out of there, learn English, go and tell their story.

'People used to say to me, "We see the lads round town." Of course that doesn't happen now' – non-white faces aren't so distinctive in Dublin any more. For the first time the East Timorese are experiencing racism in Ireland. 'Someone started to say stupid things to José at a bus stop.'

Tom Hyland grew up in Ballyfermot, the youngest of five children. Their parents had arrived in Dublin from County Westmeath in the Fifties. 'It's only now that you realize how much your parents, your mother, loved you.'

His childhood Saturdays were spent making jelly, polishing floors with rags tied to his shoes, and drinking lemonade from the corner shop. Later, as a teenager, he could drink three flagons of cider at a sitting to show he was a hard guy to the gang he was part of – 'although I hated cider and still do'. He's not much of a drinker these days. At school he excelled neither in the gym nor at his lessons. 'My sisters were the brainy ones.'

He was glad to become a bus driver. When the East Timor campaign is over he'd like to return to the buses for a few months, 'just to recapture my misspent youth'.

He was a conductor on the first bus service out to Clondalkin. His driver was a communist, called Johnny the Red. Tom and Johnny thought that the bus service to Clondalkin was a disgrace. For a working-class estate, where few people had cars, they knew that one bus leaving between eight and nine in the morning wasn't enough. Tom and Johnny the Red made their own bus corridor, with minimum publicity. They used to give up their break in order to get back out to Clondalkin from town as quickly as possible. Tom stuffed the bus with people. 'I had them hanging out of the roof. It was like sardines.'

The people of Clondalkin appreciated that Tom and Johnny were undermining the system in order to make it more efficient. Two of their passengers were ladies who worked at the Ambassador cinema. They used to give Tom and Johnny free passes for films. Tom is a big film fan. But himself and Johnny had to stop taking the passes when the two ladies started giving them the run of the Ambassador sweet kiosk as well. 'That was too much,' says Tom.

Tom had lived in the house in Ballyfermot since his parents had died – they died within days of each other. His father had a drink problem, and this sometimes manifested itself, Tom says carefully, to his mother's detriment. Tom was surprised by the grief he felt at his mother's sudden death. She died at Christmas 1981, during an unusually severe winter; at night he would dream of putting blankets on the grave. This grief at an ordinary death, and at his mother's life, is part of the reason, he thinks, why he became, in his mid-thirties, active on behalf of a country he had never heard of. 'I can't stand bullying.'

Tom had piped television in his house, which could receive the British channels. One night in 1991 a neighbour, James Hurley, asked if he could come round to watch a documentary about a massacre. Tom had a night of dominoes planned, but agreed that Jim could come. The documentary was Max Stahl's *In Cold Blood: The Massacre of East Timor*.

When it was over the Tom and James went down the Ballyfermot Road to a coin box – Tom had no phone then – and phoned the Indonesian Human Rights Campaign in London.

The words just ran out of Tom. When he was finished, 'there was this upper-class English voice on the other end saying that she couldn't understand a word I had said'.

Tom was going to hang up in a rage – 'In Ballyfermot we tend to feel a bit under siege from the other classes.' But he persisted, and the Ireland East Timor Solidarity Campaign started right there, in the phone box.

They started canvassing the relevant embassies, travelling by bus. They started picketing the relevant embassies. They were afraid they would be arrested.

They consulted a barrister who gave them this advice: 'Keep the politicians, the religious and the middle classes away from your campaign.'

Tom Hyland never forgets advice. He can still quote the advice he was given by an inspector during his training as a bus conductor: 'Always give the passenger the benefit of the doubt.'

He's worried about Ireland. The materialism and the racism weren't there when he was a boy. Maybe we're becoming less willing to help each other, he says, or to help other people.

*

Gillian Murphy is an energetic woman in a bright jumper and slacks. She is confident and frank. Her two dogs were once strays, and must think that they have died and gone to heaven. They came from the dogs' home in Rathfarnham. 'Believe me, their testicles were off in a flash,' says Gillian. 'I wanted bitches but they didn't have any.'

Three months ago the Murphys moved from the house they had lived in for twenty-five years, partly because they wanted to give their children money for a down payment on a house. This afternoon Gillian is going to look at a house for one of her daughters who is too busy to look for herself. 'She just won't get round to it,' says Gillian. Gillian is typical of her generation in that she shows extraordinary consideration for her adult children and exhibits a calm anticipation of, even a planning for, death. 'If I was left a widow I wouldn't want to stay in the old house by myself and face into the same move on my own and have to ask the kids to help me. The kids wouldn't like that.'

Gillian won't be moving again. 'Believe me,' she says. 'The woman who moved in to the old house painted the whole house yellow, which is a bit unusual, and they've torn out all the fitted wardrobes. I don't want to go back.'

The Murphys moved from Temple Gardens, off Palmerstown Road, in Dublin 6. The houses in Temple Gardens are huge, red-brick, rather ugly Victorian villas.

'Barristers bought it. It's all barristers now; they're the only people who can afford them. I think there are six of them on the road now. That good-looking Cabinet minister lives there. Yes, Liz O'Donnell,' says Gillian. 'It used to be mostly doctors.'

In 1975 Gillian and her husband, who is a doctor, paid £49,000 for their house in Temple Gardens. 'We paid the highest price ever – people were amazed. And then twenty-five years later we got the highest price ever, £1.8 million. We gave a nice party. Everyone was delighted with the price we got.'

The thing that annoyed Gillian was that there were rooms in the old house that were hardly ever used. The beautiful dining-room was never used. So she and her husband ended up living in a large house and only using the kitchen and the family room. Their main problem was finding a smaller house in the same area. The market is crowded with people over sixty-five, like the Murphys, who have sold big houses and have plenty of money to spend on somewhere smaller, which is easier to heat, more difficult to burgle and has fewer stairs.

Some aspects of the move didn't bother Gillian at all. 'I didn't mind the house being viewed. The auctioneers always gave us good warning. There are people who look at houses just out of curiosity but I don't mind that, I've been doing that myself for years. I did meals on wheels for twenty years from Beechwood church, and I'd be going into houses like the one you live in, that some old person was living in, and thinking this could be a lovely house, if it was renovated. Don't you have to go down steps to your kitchen?' I reply that indeed I do.

'But it is so stressful trying to scale down, getting the kids to come back and get all the stuff they wouldn't let you throw away, and then of course they find they don't want it themselves and they end up throwing it all into the skip. The worst part was the books. The books were all hoarded by my husband and children, they hoarded every damn thing. We gave a lot of books away. A lot of children's books. And black bags full of teddies. Geraldine was a teddy-bear collector at one time. The teddies didn't look too well after thirty years, I can tell you. They looked like they had parvo virus.'

By the time the unwanted furniture had been divided amongst the children, and three months had been spent redecorating the new house, Gillian had had enough. But she has noticed that other people are more tense than she was. 'Everyone who comes to the house to do anything, to lay a carpet and hang curtains, their faces are full of frenzy and stress.'

She likes the new house and its smaller garden. 'I'd hate the spring to come and not have a garden.'

However things are a little bit quiet on the new road. 'I know nobody in the road. But I can't complain. I was never the best for rushing in with the potted plant. Our neighbours on both sides are in their eighties. There's a young woman across here with two children of twelve and eight. The others are quite old, I suppose. I never see anyone. Everyone waves in a friendly manner. Nothing goes on. That's why these dogs are so depressed.'

*

There is a Slovak saying: 'A farmer's pride is his horse. His cow may be thin but his horse must be fat.' On Monday, 13 December 1999, the Taoiseach, Bertie Ahern, went to Armagh for the inaugural meeting of the North-South Ministerial Council. He took his entire cabinet with him, in a fleet of black Mercedes. Someone said that it looked like a Mafia funeral. Mary Holland, writing in the *Irish Times*, said: 'My own impression was of the leaders of an invading army arriving to dictate surrender terms to the defeated army. The scene was shown a number of times on BBC Northern Ireland, where viewers will have drawn their own, almost certainly tribal, conclusions.'

In Kenya, after independence, the people called the new elite the WaBenzi, because they all drove Mercedes-Benz cars.

Jack Lynch always had a Ford as his government car. When Jack Lynch was in power Ford still had an assembly plant in Cork.

In Ireland the Mercedes used to be a car for men in late middle age. In 1994 almost half of Mercedes buyers in the republic were aged between forty-five and fifty-four. Bill Duffy, head of sales for Mercedes Ireland, says: 'That's where the rich men were then.' Bill is in his late fifties. Now just a quarter of his customers are over forty-five.

The Mercedes is becoming a young man's car. In 1994 only 3 per cent of Bill's customers were aged between twenty-five and thirty-four. In 1999 this generation accounted for 22 per cent of Mercedes' trade. 'The younger generations are inheriting more. People my generation didn't get much for property. A lot of it was unsaleable ten years ago. Now you can sell well.'

Twelve years ago, in 1988, only 425 Mercedes were sold in the Republic. 'You were pushing to make sales,' says Bill Duffy. In 1999, 4,600 Mercedes were sold here and Bill's team could have shifted a lot more cars if they had had them. There is a growing demand for sports cars and convertibles, despite the weather.

'There's a new coupe in the CL class, and before it was even launched, a year before it was launched, people wanted to be the first to buy it. Our waiting-list is two years long. The car will cost about £130,000. But we have limited allocation. We'll get fifteen for the year 2000, but we could sell at least thirty a year.'

Sales went up 40 per cent in 1998 and 30 per cent in 1999. 'Sometimes I have to pinch myself. I say to myself, "Am I really alive or what is it?" Five years ago if I had predicted what is actually happening in our business now they would have put me in a straitjacket.'

Bono bought an S-class Mercedes (£64,335 to £98,900), but when it arrived the colour wasn't quite what he had expected. 'That often happens,' says Bill Duffy, 'with colour cards.' Nevertheless, Bono kept the car.

'If someone wants a silver car but buys it in green then the car isn't really what they wanted. It will be like the suit that is always at the back of the wardrobe. The dream was not fully realized.'

There is always a wait for a Mercedes, a lead time of three or four months so that a customer's choices on options like colour, type of interior, orthopaedic or heated seats and air conditioning, can be met. There are more than a hundred customer options. But now there are long waiting lists just to get to the lead time. Demand far exceeds supply. Ireland is the fastest-growing Mercedes market in Europe. Bill is up every morning at five o'clock to go to the gym.

Bill Duffy sits in the 1950s Mercedes building, so beautiful that it is listed, in an office that Doris Day could walk right into at any moment. Bill's office has a huge parlour palm, a huge yucca tree, beige walls, glass shelving, two aerial views of the Mercedes plants in Germany and two reproductions of vintage Mercedes posters – one showing a couple driving through European mountains, oblivious to the dark skier diving over their car.

'A lot of what you get you can't see,' says Bill Duffy.

In Ireland, 'the biggest selling car is not the smallest car'. More than a third of the Mercedes sold in Ireland are the E-class models, which cost more than £35,000.

People buy a Mercedes for different reasons. 'A lot of it is emotional. We have this argument with the German people. Their ads have always been based on technology, but now the word hedonism is coming in. If you're buying something like the SLK, the hedonism factor has to be high. People like the way they look in the car, they like the way they think they look in the car.'

If a customer decides he wants to buy a Jaguar, Bill won't try to stop him. 'I prefer a guy to get it out of his system.'

The Mercedes is a big car in a self-conscious culture. 'Sometimes a man or woman is extremely successful in business and they want one. You know what stops them? "What will my customers think?"'

Mercedes were brought to Ireland by Stephen O'Flaherty, who got the concession for them just after the war. O'Flaherty started off in Townshend Street. He also sold Volkswagen Beetles. O'Flaherty then moved premises to Shelbourne Road in Ballsbridge, coincidentally next to the old Swastika Laundry. My auntie Rosemary, then a single girl just back from America, bought a beige Volkswagen Beetle there in the Sixties. It was her first car. It had a special compartment at the back, behind the passenger seats, for transporting one's nieces. Auntie Rosemary had a small beige plaque made which said, 'This car belongs to Rose Mary Brady.' Rose Mary was how Americans said Rosemary. I thought: 'One day I will have a Volkswagen Beetle.'

*

There is a wooden sign on the way to the toilets in Cork airport that reads: 'Small airport, big heart.' It is a heart-shaped sign; Cork airport is a literal-minded place. There is also a life-sized statue of Jack Charlton in Cork airport, which sits beside the carp pond just behind the glass lift, and looks just like Jack Charlton.

There is a statue of the hurler Christy Ring at Cork airport, but his boots are wrong. Christy should be wearing the high boots of his time, but the sculptor has given him dainty soccer pumps. 'It's not his fault,' says my uncle. 'The fellow who did it is too young to know that.'

The wooden sign should read, 'Small airport, big fog,' because Cork airport is frequently shrouded in a blanket of mist. This doesn't affect the departing flights quite so much as the incoming, which frequently cannot land. Like this morning, for example. The 7 a.m. flight from Dublin, which is to become the 8.30 flight EI 032 to Dublin, was due in at 8, but there won't be another announcement about it until 9, and in the end we do not actually leave until 10.45. Flight JY 883 from Birmingham, due in to Cork at 8.25, is diverted to Kerry, which is ignominious for Cork people, and means a three-hour coach trip for the passengers. Flight BA 7841 from Manchester, due in at 8.10, is in a holding pattern. There are three flights to and from Manchester each day.

Cork airport was built on a hill, and nobody understands why, although there are rumours of political intervention.

'Every time I drive up the hill, I think: this is a great place for an airport,' says Anne O'Leary sarcastically. She works for Esat Telecom and travels to Dublin all the time. She's on the seven o'clock flight this morning 'The 8.30 flight is booked out. I think it's a smaller plane.'

For the return journey from Dublin to Cork there is an Aer Aran flight at 16.25, an Aer Lingus flight at 18.30 and another at 22.10. 'At least you can go out after work then,' says Anne O'Leary.

Niall Daly flies to Heathrow every Monday on the 7.30, and flies back every Friday night on the 19.10. 'Fog really affects arrivals,' he says. He's wearing jeans and t-shirt and is a director with a waste-disposal company. He lived and worked in London for fifteen years. Now he lives in Lismore, in west

Waterford. He leaves the house at 5.45 each Monday, and it takes him fifty minutes to get to the airport. By 8.45 he's in the middle of the London rush hour. 'It can be a bit of a shock to the system,' he says. 'But I'll keep going in the short term at least. No, in the medium term.' Every week he sees lots of the same faces on his commute.

Pat Herne works for a company called EC, which provides computer technology for data storage to banks, and flies once or twice a month. EC's London office is located near Heathrow. A lot of companies are re-locating there now, Pat says. If he succeeds in getting his bags from baggage reclaim in Heathrow by 9 o'clock – 'Terminal One is the other end of nowhere' – then he can be in the office anywhere between 9.30 and 10.45. Pat will be there for a week of hotel living. 'It's okay, but it's monotonous. I train at night and my boss is over there so I'll probably go drinking as well.' He doesn't mind any of this. It's Cork airport that he minds. Very much.

'This airport was supposed to be built in east Cork, where it's flat. It's the only airport in Europe that is built on a hill. The only good thing about it is that our company has two private jets, which Aer Rianta puts up and provides hangars for. They're for customers.

'No flight I ever get from here is empty. The front of the plane [where a lot of business passengers sit] is full. The only thing I do know is that it is the same in America. I know guys who have terrible trouble getting flights there. The Americans don't mind travelling. They say 'It's my job'. You do get used to it, you just don't notice, you know. Most people don't notice, you know. I actually enjoy flying, so.'

*

Ferdinand Sauza lives on the North Circular Road. His landlord is 'oldest people, Irish nice people. He understand everything. If I don't have rent he say, "O'kay, later."'

At the moment Ferdinand is working on a site in Howth, building houses and apartments. They'll sell, he says, for £700,000 or £1 million. 'Oh, it is beautiful,' he says. His building mates call him Fred. He wants it made very clear that he is officially employed, and that he pays his taxes.

Ferdinand Sauza arrived in Dublin in the container of a lorry. He didn't know who was driving it, or where he was going. The driver of the lorry only opened the container at night, to let Ferdinand out to relieve himself. He released him into O'Connell Street in the middle of the night. 'I just drop down in Dublin,' says Ferdinand. 'Now I am free.'

The trip had cost Ferdinand's friends about 4,000 deutschmarks. He had come from Macedonia, but was from Jakova in northern Kosovo.

Ferdinand is an only child, and in Jakova he ran a small shop, selling cigarettes and vegetables, to support himself and his parents. Plainclothes Serbian policemen used to come around, he says, grab money out of the till and break the place up. 'He have gun, he have everything.'

One day, Ferdinand says, he sort of cracked. He hit the policemen. Two friends took him to Macedonia by car. They knew that if he stayed in Kosovo he would be killed by the police. Of the four close friends Ferdinand had in Kosovo, three are now dead and one is missing. They had gone to school together, they were the same age as him – thirty-two.

When he arrived in Dublin, Ferdinand slept 'on boxes' for six or seven nights. One night on O'Connell Street Ferdinand heard two guys speaking Albanian. That night he slept under the Daniel O'Connell statue. The next morning the two guys brought him to register at the Department of Justice. For two months Ferdinand stayed in a B&B in Swords. 'The boss of the hotel,' says Ferdinand, 'he look after me. He included me. I am different country.'

Ferdinand was badly beaten up in Swords. He was sitting in the local pub, where he knew the bouncer. 'I was on my first pint. My first pint,' says Ferdinand in wonder. 'These three guys come up to me and say, "Where you from?" I say I am from Kosovo. They say, "What the fuck are you doing here?"'

The three men started to hit him, even though the bouncer of the pub tried to protect him. 'He held me like this and said "Don't hate him, don't hate him",' says Ferdinand.

Later an old woman found him, beaten, on the street and called an ambulance. She was the woman who cleaned the B&B where he was staying.

'A very, very nice woman. I said to her, "I didn't do nothing." She said "I know that. Maybe one day it'll happen to me as well."'

Ferdinand says he was arrested in the hospital. The lawyer appointed to the case said, according to Ferdinand, 'Forget about it. No one listen to you, refugee.'

On Saturday Ferdinand works till lunchtime, goes home to have a shower, then comes into town for a drink. He usually goes home about seven o'clock on a Saturday evening. 'After seven o'clock loads of people are drunk. You're from another country ...'

When asked what he thinks of Irish women, Ferdinand is tactful. 'They speak like men. In Kosovo society is more traditional. You don't meet men for one night. But everything is okay, you enjoying yourself.'

He broke up with his Irish girlfriend, although her parents were welcoming to him. He went to their home in Carlow and brought gifts. They gave him gifts. There were no problems.

'But sometimes I can't take anymore. I can't enjoy the coffee,' he looks down at his coffee, 'I can't enjoy the pint. People say, "Look at her, look at him." Most Irish people are good, but perhaps it's better to live away from here.'

*

Una O'Sullivan is looking for commercial work, because designing one-off houses is so time-consuming. But one-off houses are her bread and butter. People want what they are familiar with, an exact replica of what they've seen. 'Sometimes people come in with a photograph of what they want and you can't deviate from that. What comes out of this office, an awful lot of it is dormer bungalows. I wouldn't be absolutely happy about that.'

Una O'Sullivan is an architect in Bandon, County Cork. Her secretary, Svetlana O'Carroll, is from Moscow. Svetlana married an Irish man. 'We're quite lucky to be renting in Drimoleague,' says Svetlana, who is blonde, wearing trendy glasses and a patterned shirt, and is leaving the office for the day. She misses a lot about Russia. 'Everything, everything,' she says.

Una lives with her mother, who is a widow, in a house on Haig's Terrace which, like her office, has a shopfront: 'We had a shop at one time.' She's bought a site near Schull, but has had no time to design anything for it. She's also bought an old school house in Bandon. 'But that was for family reasons. My father taught there at one time.'

Una's offices are beside McLaughlin's farm suppliers and opposite the Methodist church (Sunday Service 11.30 a.m.). Her building used to be a souvenir shop. Una's older brothers and sisters used to buy single cigarettes here. The owner lived upstairs. Una thinks she went to live with her boyfriend, although she is quite elderly.

The shop front, now painted a tasteful navy, encourages people to just walk in. 'That's the horrific part. Mondays and Fridays are the worst. Monday's mart day and on Friday everyone comes into town to do their business.' Today is Friday.

Bandon is like a dream of the ideal town. A river really does run through it. The new fast road from Cork goes under the old railway viaduct, over which bowlers used to attempt to lob cast-iron balls. Bandon was a strongly Protestant town, and still looks like one, most of the time. The basket of the old delivery bike outside the butcher's is now filled with flowers. The chemist shops are called medical halls. The Curtain Hall is above the video shop, in a fine terraced building. At the tailor's, the navy glazed cotton blinds, which any architect might be proud of, are drawn. The shop has closed down.

The front window on the right of the tailor's shopfront still has a packet of classic pyjamas in paisley for only £10, and wool nylon longjohns for £23.50. Someone moved fast. There is an application for planning permission on the door of the tailor's, from a woman with a local address. She wants to open a café with a toilet block and bakery extension.

In the library in Bandon Shopping Centre, Brenda and Fiona say that *Tara Road* is their most popular book. In nonfiction, Peter Mayle's *One Year in Provence* is the most popular. There's a new shopping centre planned for Bandon, on the river.

'Holiday homes wouldn't be the tenth of it,' says Una O'Sullivan. There's a greenbelt round Cork city now, and people are moving out further and further. 'The likes of Kinsale has gone stupid in terms of the price of property.' From Bandon, on the new road, you can get to the south side of Cork in twenty minutes and to the north side in less than forty. Bandon has recently been designated a special development area. This gives builders a 50 per cent tax write-off for the next two years.

'People are assessing what they have and deciding whether to sell,' says Una. 'There should have been a master plan, because the sites along the river are a bit bitty. They'll probably go for apartments.'

She says this type of designation is not the best thing for a town. It's not a natural way for a town to develop. Clonakilty was developed in this way as a seaside tourist utility. 'A particularly horrific idea, really. The beds are empty down there for the guts of the year.'

Una designs big houses. 'Fifteen hundred square feet is very small house now. Twenty-five hundred square feet is what people are pitching at.' People want four bedrooms, walk-in wardrobes, *en suite* bathrooms – two per house – two living-rooms, a dining-room, a utility room, kitchen and pantry.

'Pantry is a big buzzword now. If you've a pantry you're made.'

I myself would like a pantry, very much.

In three years of private practice Una has only had two or three couples who were open to the idea of a modern house. 'If you show most people a modern elevation, they don't understand it.'

*

It's difficult to open a bank account in Ireland, if you are only recently arrived.

You have to present your passport, a utility bill addressed to you, and a reference from a foreign bank. These rules are designed, says Fergus Hopper, the manager of AIB in O'Connell Street, to prevent money-laundering. Unfortunately, such vigilance was not always applied to Irish people opening non-resident accounts, but we'll let that pass.

Fergus's friends call him Dennis. The majority of the people coming into the branch are Irish, although it does have foreign customers. On the whole, though, the people coming in can be divided into two categories, says Fergus. Passing traffic, which is largely working class. Many of these customers live locally in Dublin 1, or work there, although there is one man who has lived in Dalkey for fifty years and still banks in O'Connell Street. The second category are corporate and commercial customers, like the Irish recruitment agency which is bringing people in from America to work here. Or the hotel managers, shop assistants and big companies like Eircom.

In the smoking section of the staff canteen there is a paperback copy of *The Fires of Heaven*, which is Book Five of the 'Wheels of Time' series. There is a copy of *U* magazine. In the ladies' lavatory there is a nailbrush on one of the four sinks, and assorted shoes for long days. Everything is so orderly and quiet that you want to work here, in this building that was once the Dawson bookshop and overlooks the statue of Parnell, the Rotunda hospital and the old Ambassador cinema.

The first foreign customer is Chinese. He's eighteen years old. The little girl with him, whose English name is Grace, is just seventeen. They are both very pretty.

'At first I want to go to America,' says the boy. 'Many Chinese people there. If you come here you must pay a lot of money. £20,000. I come to study English at the College of English and if I collect enough money I go to university. But not here. University here not very good and very expensive. Nobody in China know Irish university. Maybe Canada. Maybe Australia. Also very expensive. I came just one month. I'm from north China. From Dairen city, very beautiful. It is Hong Kong of the north.

'A lot of tall building. A lot of park. A lot of people in house. Apartment. Five million people. This city very small.'

How does he find Dublin otherwise?

'Not very well. Weather not very good and traffic not very well. I have a flat in Raheny, also I find a job in McDonald's. I go back to China because China need some business person. China change a lot. If you have a lot of money you can go to another country. Maybe ten years, maybe twenty years, big change come in China. We hope it. We wish it. My father is a business man, yes, international business man.

'Our big dream to go to university. We are sleeping a little time, I work six day a week, one day for nine hours. I get £4.25 for one hour.

'We go to Alpha College of English, in North Great George's Street. Do you know it?'

I do not.

This seems to confirm his worst suspicions. 'No one know

it. College is £4,000 and passport and visa is rest of £20,000. We pay that to a Chinese person who arrange for us.

'Irish people very friendly. Some children, fourteen, thirteen years old not very friendly. But people over twenty very friendly. For two week I stay with family. For long time I can't find house. The house in Raheny very bad, badder than my Chinese house, old and dirty with just a washing-machine. Five people in three bedroom.

'Today I wanted a banker's card but I need letter from my headmaster. In China a lot of people, maybe all the people, keep money in the bank.'

He plans to stay in Ireland for one or two years before moving on. Altogether he will be away from China for about ten years.

Cesar is from Lisbon. He came for a holiday two years ago and fell in love with Ireland. Yes, he did. Then he came back three months ago and started looking for a job. For the past month has been a security man in the Parnell Centre car park. He works in information and at the controls of the other security men. He has only one day in the week off and on that day 'I go to city to pubs and clubs. I enjoy it.'

'I like Dublin very much. The people are very polite. I don't know why I like it but I do. I want to stay in Ireland, get married, have a nice family. Children. I'm happy.

'In Lisbon it is much more difficult. My parents are working but there is a lot of unemployment. I have one sister.'

Debbie, from Zimbabwe, likes Dublin too. 'I love the array

of food and so many people and the libraries and the galleries.'
She met her Irish husband in Zimbabwe when he was an aid
worker. After they moved to Dublin, she went for a job as a
receptionist at an outreach programme for HIV positive people, and ended up getting a job as a counsellor. He would like
to move somewhere else in Europe, perhaps, but Debbie likes
Dublin: 'It's very easy.' At first she lived with her husband in
Limerick. 'Limerick is very insular. People can't open up. I felt
very isolated. Here there's an easier atmosphere. Most people
in Limerick call me a refugee. Travellers hit really hard on you.'

*

Catherine Atkins has worked at the O'Connell Street branch of
the AIB bank for thirty-six years. She's a slight woman with
short hair and the clear, considered way of talking that has now
gone out of fashion. Her accent is hard to place. It isn't the
country (she's from Tipperary) and it isn't the town. As soon as
you speak to her you know that Catherine Atkins is wide awake.

Catherine Atkins works on the counter in the bank, and
pretty well always has. It was about six years ago that the number of foreign customers increased dramatically, she says.

'They were paid by Eastern Health Board cheques initially,
and at that time we looked after EHB cheques. We used to look
after those local people who came from Summerhill. The
cheques were issued by the EHB in Summerhill. They were so
deprived.'

But suddenly, it seemed, five years ago a new queue appeared at the bank. 'We used to call it the foreign queue. On Mondays, Tuesdays and Wednesdays we used to wonder had we any other customers than those who were of African origin.

'I remember a customer saying to me that it was wonderful, to see this mix of people in Ireland. Irish people are very parochial. I'm parochial.

'We were afraid to cause problems by asking too many questions. I'd have an African person in front of me and I had to have information. But I was afraid to be racist, which was silly. Now we're much more in command.

'I think the media influenced us,' she bows her head slightly in my direction. 'And people were confrontational on their [the foreigners'] side. Allegedly there were big scams going on. We were very fussy about what we'd cash and wouldn't cash. A classic case would be the way, in a lot of cultures, people have three names. They take on the name of the grandfather or of the grandmother. So that would make my name Catherine O'Connor Atkins, but perhaps there was only Catherine O'Connor on the cheque. O'Connor was my grandmother's name, and the bank wouldn't cash that cheque for me. Because fraud goes on in a bank at huge levels. Or the writing on the cheque was a problem, getting names wrongly written. People in the EHB were over-worked and getting the names wrong. They got very busy.

'My basic instinct was to feel sorry for people who have to go and face someone like me looking for information. I spent so much time on the phone to the Eastern Health Board. Before you could give a description of Mary Smith and they could confirm that it was her, because that person was a regular. It was very difficult starting all the time with new people.

'Say now, and I'll be killed for saying this, I find Irish people are racist. They crack jokes behind the scenes. To some extent I wouldn't be at fault so much, but then I started to ask myself when I was dealing with an African man, "Have I actually got the same respect for him that I'd have for one of the regular business customers whom I know well?" And I wasn't very happy with my response. Not very proud.

'This was a sudden influx and I remember a time that if you saw an African in the office he was bound to be a doctor. And some people were quite confrontational and a few people like that give everyone a bad name. ID cards with photographs were often incomplete or in the wrong name.

'We were much more cautious dealing with someone who wasn't Irish. They'd be upset because you were looking at them very intently. It was unfamiliar. Yet there was no problem getting the right ID from someone who is white.

'It was the numbers. There were so many. It was endless. I'm dealing with gangsters down there every day of my life. You wouldn't believe what's going on, what went on twenty years ago.

'You have to remember it was very élitist to have a bank account even in the Sixties. Even my parents. My father had an account. Women were waiting for these gods to come home and give them money. And women accepted this, stupidly.

'It was only when keeping money on the premises became a security risk for employers that they encouraged staff to open bank accounts. It was cheaper for the employers than hiring security. I remember when there were charges on opening bank accounts, when the first Corporation workers opened accounts, the first building workers.

'Now the customers are not as in awe of the bank, and that's a very good thing. They know their rights more and they question more. There was a time when people used to get dressed up to come into the bank. I know an old lady who still does that, even though she doesn't even see the manager.

'The management roles have altered. There used to be the manager, the accountant, and the number-one cashier. When I started work the number-one cashier was an awesome figure. But there were advantages to that because it was more personal in a way. A manager could lend you money on his own assessment of you. He just knew instinctively if you were all right, so if someone had a bit of go in them he'd lend you money.

'Now everything is on facts and figures. It's not what you sound like to the manager – it's all on paper. It's safe. It's not allowing for someone who'll have a go of something. I'd a friend, an actor in the Gate. His contact with me was very important to him. I could say that he was all right for two hundred pounds.

'It's ranks now, and hierarchy. I genuinely think that Fergus, who is our manager, is nearest the old-style manager.

'I came up in 1963 from Tipperary. It was my first job. I was eighteen. The innocence of it. Living in the Fifties was rather like living in the middle ages. I remember the Beatles at the Adelphi. Women weren't allowed on the counter. We were stuck with the donkey work. It wasn't the done thing to see a woman on the counter. All the women have to have uniforms and the reason the women had uniforms was so as not to upset the men, sexually. When I think of it now.

'After about six years some of us asked for a transfer, but I was told it was just a phase. Maybe it's the bank's fault. I would have done better if I'd moved. You saw that man I was talking to in the canteen. He's an assistant manager and he started six months after me. I could have fought like hell. But I think if your ambitions aren't met in the first ten years, if you know in the first ten years that there isn't a snowball's chance of getting on, you lose a bit of your drive. Myself and another girl were put on Scale 3, which was a stepping stone to SBO [Senior Branch Officer], which I am now. She was a very ambitious woman from Waterford and she fought like hell to get on. She's quite a senior manager today. Women had to be twice as good as men. By the mid-Seventies the bank was obliged to improve because some of the girls wanted to get on, so the bank appointed women to be assistant managers. One woman who became an assistant manager then was the age I am now. I thought she was ancient.

'Now the staff are totally different, and much more casual in simple things, like calling customers by their first names. I'd be going down through the floor listening to them, because they don't stand on ceremony for customers. In the bank strike of the Seventies I got a job as a chambermaid in London and I had an account in a bank on the Edgeware Road in London. I remember being stunned by the attitude of the girls on the counter – they were half-talking to friends as they served customers. I was quite ashamed of working in a bank when I saw them.

'Now our staff are so young when they go on the counter. I marvel at them sometimes. I'd ask them, "Why did you cash that?" And they say, "Oh, I know his brother."

'They're really quite brave, although they're not as respectful. It's a different era. They're such nice kids. A lot of the old work has been eliminated by technology, by 24-hour banking, the ATM machine. It's a world of plastic.

'People won't be coming into the office. It'll also cost the banks less, because their staff costs are their biggest costs. But everyone needs to talk to someone. Soon there'll be no interaction at all.

'I love my contact with the customers. I'd have a lot of older people. They come in to do business in town, they come in to the bank. In the old days, this bank was really at the beginning of the city.

'You can't blame a generation like our parents, but people now are intolerant too. I remember being in the canteen, talking about the gay issue, and I would be appalled by their ignorance.

'Being single I've moved around more and I've seen more. I can see intolerance in myself in some thngs. But I can't stand sniggering at anything different to what is considered to be Irish and "normal".

'I've an English friend who lives here and I'd tell her about the Nigerians coming here and she'd say, "So what? It's great." It's to do with our parochial upbringing. It's that kind of thing.

'I try to treat all the customers all the same. I wish I felt the same. It's not right to do all the right things and say all the right things. It's feeling the right things that's important. When you've reached your maturity, the maturity to realize that ultimately you're no better than anyone else. That's the ideal. I don't want to think that people would say in the queue "Don't go to her, she questions too much." I think I'm fairly okay with the customers. Including little batches of fellas who would be as high as kites.'

*

The car park at Tallaght hospital has 500 spaces and four floors. Peter Keegan is its manager. Peter is just about to move house. He never expected, he says, to be living in a £300,000 house.

Tallaght was the first hospital car park to charge more than one flat rate. 'Beaumont hospital has gone the same. St James' are finding that people are parking their cars at the hospital, paying one pound for the day. And then walking into town.'

If you leave the Tallaght hospital car park within twenty minutes of entering, you park for free. Then it's £1.50 per hour up to a maximum of £5. But the thing is that you never know in Tallaght hospital car park. 'We take everything subjectively. It's the social aspect, because it's a hospital. A&E, that's the problem. It's not a shopping centre. It's not the same psyche at all. People are under stress. The last thing they want is me to be officious. Do I like it? Well, I'm good at it. I like dealing with people. I've been working in car parks for five years.'

Peter has worked in the car parks at Drury Street, ILAC shopping centre, Irish Life, Arnotts, Parnell Street and Bray. 'In Arnotts and Dawson Street you get better-educated people. At Arnotts they say, "Here's my card. I'll be writing in to complain." It'd wreck your head.'

This car park is newer and brighter than the others. 'But you're out in the wilds. There's a constant wind, even in summer. It's the middle of nowhere.'

There are 130 spaces on every floor. Each space measures 2.1 metres in width, except the wheelchair spaces which are a car and a half wide. Disabled parking can cause problems for the managers of car parks. 'The Wheelchair Society of Ireland are a pressure group with many good people, and then some people with serious chips,' says Peter resignedly. 'They only want people with stickers to use the spaces, but this is a hospital ...' The hospital is strict about handing out parking validation to relatives. For example, the wife of a patient will be allowed to park for nothing, but not his children.

The car park was built by private investors. The hospital didn't sell the land to the developers and as soon as they've recouped enough money the car park will revert to the hospital. 'The operator has all the pain.'

Peter's office is next to the two pay stations, so he has more contact with the customers. There are three staff on during the day, and one at night. Two security men work twelve-hour shifts. Everything is on a timelock and there are cash pick-ups two or three times a week. It's a lot of trouble to go to for an unstoppable flow of cars, and the emotions that surround them.

'People lose their road sense in a car park. It's like they lose confidence. They drive up the down ramp. They just don't read the signs.' The ramps in this car park are narrow – 'at least they give people the perception that they are narrow, and that the turn is too tight. They get nervy. You're talking about people who are stressed anyway.' Later, I disgrace myself on a ramp.

Peter doesn't think much of cars. 'They're a status system, a sign of independence. And people are willing to pay the cost of maintaining their cars, no matter what. In twenty or thirty years driving is going to go the road of smoking. It'll be seen as anti-social to use a car to get to work. It'll be, "He's what? He's driving in!" It'll be frowned on.

'You can't drive down the residential road where I used to live because all the maisonettes have two cars apiece. Ten years ago that wouldn't even have been one car apiece.

'One Saturday it took five hours to get out of the car park at the College of Surgeons. All the down ramps were blocked. You need to get twenty or thirty cars out at a time to get a flow going. There was serious traffic on the road outside, and the whole place just gridlocked.'

'They've extractor fans in the ILAC now, the cashiers have to have fresh air pumped in. If you don't have that you get nausea, headaches, irritability.

'The one thing that messes us up is the mobile phone. Once you've paid you have fifteen minutes to get out. Now people go back to their cars, take a call or make a call, and then their time has expired. It's in the psyche not to pay. You say, "Put a pound in the slot," and they say, "What slot?"'

*

Read's is a photocopying shop on Nassau Street in Dublin which charges 3p per copy on white paper, 4p with staff service. It is extremely busy, perhaps because it gives out a free re-fill pad with every 100 copies you make. The most frequent cry in Read's is 'Next please'.

Here's some of what was photocopied in Read's between about 11.30 and 12.30 one Wednesday.

1) A 20-page draft of a history of the Carden family, who left Ireland to go to Australia in 1830.

2) Thirty timetables for a beauty salon.

3) Two hundred copies of a chapter from a sociology book.

4) All the correspondence involved in a complaint being made to An Post about the late delivery of a parcel. 'Normally I'm not a complainer,' says the woman. 'But now I'm sending all of this to the Ombudsman.'

4) 120 copies of the dinner menu and 120 copies of the lunch menu from the Rubicon restaurant. Copies made by Darren from Limerick.

5) *General Principles of EU Law* – the young student won't give her name.

6) Unspecified number of sales descriptions of handbags, by a man in a hurry. 'I've got to go, I'm late for a meeting. We can't get any craft workers. Everyone's being re-trained. All the skilled workers are gone.'

7) Leaflets written by Kitty Leung 'for my little home-based business based on natural aloe vera products'.

8) 140 pages of a doctoral thesis on the eighteenth-century middle class, with an analysis of their good manners. 'My main witness is Frances Burney.' The author of the thesis is a young Breton woman. She's also teaching in Trinity and in her final year studying Stategic Management and Business Policy. Two degrees at the same time? 'In another few years I wouldn't be so arrogant.'

9) The first five chapters of a textbook for the Christmas test in business studies in Trinity. The boy won't give his name. 'I don't want to buy it. The lecturer wrote the book and put it on the course material so we have to buy it. They're all at it.'

10) 136 copies of something private, by Sarah.

11) Hundreds and hundreds and hundreds of copies made

by an Australian woman who is so small that she has to stand on a pile of papers to work comfortably on the machine. 'This is the chepeast place in Ireland to photocopy. It's worth the train fare from Mullingar. I'm doing £150 worth of copies. It's a campaign work, against the media. To get the media to tell the truth as opposed to lies.

'You could say me and my husband were ethnically cleansed in Dún Laoghaire. We lived there for twelve years, in a one-bedroom flat for which we paid £300 per month. Overnight the landlord put it up to £450. We had to move to where rent was cheaper.'

12) Copies of a business report on an assignment for the Dublin Business School in Aungier Street, by Sanvara, who arrived two months ago from Karachi.

13) An unspecified number of pages from a microbiology textbook, copied by Haffix Hussaein who is in fourth med, and misses the much faster pace of Kuala Lumpur.

The fourteen black and white and two colour photocopying machines in Read's are serviced by Jason Redmond every 70,000 copies. Jason works for Canon and is from Sallynoggin.

'Canon are well established. They won the Excellence Through People Award. I didn't just want a factory job, I wanted a career. It's a very open company, and I want to travel with them. I want to go to America. I'll start off in Boston.'

5
[talking]

Eircom Park is made of bone-white plastic and surrounded by tiny trees, which look like parsley stalks stuck into the ground. There is a long low building to the left of the stadium, with a glass roof. 'That'll be the kit room,' says Claire Kavanagh, who is the receptionist behind a high desk at the FAI headquarters in Merrion Square. Claire handles 'twelve incoming lines by thirty extensions', she tells you. When she's not answering phone calls she is an enthusiastic spokesperson for the Football Association. If only they'd put her in charge of ticket distribution.

Adjacent to the main stadium, which also has a glass roof, there are two ordinary-sized pitches. 'There's going to be about ten of them, eventually,' says Claire. 'The stadium has a retractable pitch. Would you like me to demonstrate that for you?'

I say I would like that very much. I had gone looking for

Eircom Park in the offices of Eircom on Stephen's Green, where it had been sitting on a piece of blue baize in the corner of the lobby, amongst the leather couches, the bright rugs and the wood and glass coffee tables. But that Eircom Park now resided in the RDS, unretrieved after the Ireland v. Yugoslavia game. Claire has the second model. She calls a young man called Cathal to come and plug it in. 'It's a great toy,' he says.

Cathal hits the red switch marked 'lights'. He hits the black switch marked 'pitch'. The three of us watch attentively as the main pitch slides out of the stadium, into the gap between the two practice pitches.

'Deadly, isn't it?' says Claire. 'That'll take approximately four hours in real life. And the roof of the stadium will take approximately twenty-five minutes to retract.'

'The roof won't be glass,' says Cathal. The black switch marked 'roof' is broken. 'When it's closed it will create a black box effect. It'll seat 45,000 with a good view.'

'HBG are in charge of construction,' says Claire. 'RHWL are the architects. It's based on the model of Arnhem stadium in Holland. It's the same guys who designed Coventry City. It's fully supported. That means it's fully supported, it's not looking for funding.'

The question is, where will it be located? Where exactly is CityWest? 'I don't know myself,' says Cathal. 'Somewhere off the Naas dual carriageway. I don't think there's anything out there yet. It's a pretty bland name.'

Claire is phoning upstairs, checking her information. 'It's

about Eircom Park. Am I right in saying that there'll be parking spaces for three thousand cars? And that the pitch will take four hours to retract? And that the roof will take twenty-five minutes?'

A glass cabinet in the alcove of the reception areas is full of trophies. Under-16 European Championship Winner, Under-18 Championship Winner, Nordic Cup Winner, Under-16. Not one trophy is dated later than 1998. A jewel-encrusted soccer ball sits in a sort of vase. 'That was a presentation by UEFA,' says Claire 'to us.'

It seemed rude to ask what it was presented for. Experts can be touchy about ignorance. Cathal unplugs the model and retires. Claire phones Philippa Haines, who is handling the PR for Eircom Park. Philippa sounds English, and very tired. I'd rather talk to Claire. 'I'm from Tallaght myself so it'd suit me, being out that way,' she says. 'It's very exciting for all of us. Especially for those who've been involved for years. The men. Who've gone now. Who've died. Good afternoon, Football Association.'

She fields the call. 'Arsenal are my team. I'm an Arsenal girl. Awkward. The boyfriend is Man United.'

Like Bertie, I say. Like the Taoiseach. He supports Man United.

'Yes,' says Claire. She fields this as well. 'So we have killings. Killings,' she says.

*

Brendan is the director of information technology for a large company, and has a 5-series BMW and a Rado watch. He's in his mid-thirties, slightly plump, and he's worked for huge companies all his life. 'I'm head-hunted once a fortnight, not necessarily within Ireland.'

Brendan likes Fridays best, because he can dress casually then. 'I dress West Coast casual. It softens you up for the weekend. Suddenly, it's Welcome to America. We wear Timberland shoes, Ralph Lauren sportswear, all labels, subtle but highly visible. You can lean back further in the chair when your collar is open. Friday actually is lethal. There's nothing worse than being the boss and discovering that someone's better dressed than you. More people get fired on a Friday than on any other day, did you know that?'

The happier Brendan seems the unhappier he talks, perhaps to please me. 'What's a cosmopolitan city? It's a bullshit term for a dump. For a place where no one will talk to you.'

'The problem in Ireland is that the number of IT people is going down. Business is being led by IT now, and it's a huge con job from start to finish. Businesses are taking advice from IT people whose only aim is to build up their own skills and marketability. Of course that means that they encourage their bosses to buy in systems simply because they need experience on those systems. It's a very, very, very dirty business.

'We were looking for an IT security policy system, with double verification, etc. We brought in two of the big five management consultants, looking for a relatively simple, boilerplate set of policies. Not one of them could do that for me. It would have been worth about two days' charge to them. They told us they couldn't just produce the policies, they'd have to do a full business analysis, for God's sake. Listen, the consultant's job on a Monday is to get Tuesday's business. To create smoke and mirrors around analysis is to their benefit. They make millions from it.'

Now Brendan won't consult management consultants at all. 'If I'm investigating a system I'll go and ask other companies who have installed it. I'll ask them, 'Did it do what it says on the tin?' Companies will share with each other. They'll share everything except an absolute failure.'

*

Polly Young-Eisendrath has the body of a boy, with slightly rounded shoulders, and that tight American look: perfect short haircut, nude make-up and small earrings. Her little navy jacket has slightly shiny buttons, and could be a velvet mix. Underneath she wears a collarless white top. Her long dark grey skirt is split up the side, and clings to her flat stomach. Only her shoes, which are square-toed slip-ons with a slightly child-like look to them, betray the fact that she is not a high-ranking executive with a major corporation. As she talks she gestures with her glasses, which she holds in her left hand in an authoritative way. She could be a Patricia Cornwell heroine. She is a Jungian analyst.

At breaktime the corridors are crowded, and it feels like school. It is Saturday and the Milltown Institute, once a seminary, is housing several courses and workshops, hosted by the Irish School of Homeopathists, the Irish Institute of Counselling and Hypnotherapy and the Irish Institute of Kinesiologists. The coffee-break crowd is overwhelmingly female. In one corridor stand a blonde woman in a leather jacket and an older, balding man. They are looking down at four pieces of paper the man has arranged on the floor. The blonde woman is thinking. Each piece of paper has a word written on it. Reading clockwise from the top left hand corner the words are Safety, Development, Angst and Fear. The man is looking at the blonde woman, waiting for a suggestion. The man is saying something like 'It doesn't really work, does it?' Human development is a tough busineses.

But we are only sweeping by, back to Polly's lecture, which is entitled 'Hothouse Mothering and the Divine Child'. According to José, 'Hothouse Mothering and the Divine Child' has attracted the highest number of people who have ever attended one of these talks, which are hosted by the Irish Analytical Psychology Association. José, who is from Brazil, is on the IAPA's committee. He had been impossible to reach the day before. 'My answering machine was jammed with calls,' he says. All ten copies of Polly Young-Eisendrath's book, *Women and Desire*, have been sold.

'It was at a very good price,' says José. 'Fifteen pounds for a hardback. It will be much more expensive in the shops.' He has a therapist's lack of embarrassment about money.

It is Polly Young-Eisendrath's theory that full-time mothering, and a mother's total absorption in her child, is very bad for both. 'It produces a child that is narcissistic and self-interested with a false view of their own importance,' she told Kathryn Holmquist of the *Irish Times*. 'Most of the psychopathology I see in my practice is as a result of a child being trapped with a lone woman and having to take on her emotional needs without any siblings to help spread the pressure.'

Here is a message guaranteed to give working mothers a brief break in their diet of guilt. It doesn't look like the executive mothers are here this morning – probably too busy, or too tired. The audience is a good deal untidier than Polly. Their hair is wilder. They have stomachs that are not flat, and Saturday shoes: flat sandals with tights, runners, comfortable lace-ups. There are a lot of cardigans, and not much make up. There are between sixty and seventy people in the room – about twenty will go on this afternoon to a workshop Polly is running for psychotherapists – and most are taking notes.

It is strange to be sitting in what feels like a school with a class full of mothers. You can feel the swirl of the normal Saturday – swimming lessons, supermarkets, football practice, ballet classes, barbecues, pocket money and the long wait in the car at a discreet distance from the disco during what is Dublin's third rush hour, which takes place well after midnight – all of this postponed and re-scheduled this morning, waiting for them beyond the gates of Milltown Park. Polly Young-

Eisendrath is talking about the two varieties of the adult narcissist: the benign narcissist, who takes in his mother's idealized vision of him, and sails through things and people; and the malignant narcissist, who is filled with a great deal of rage.

'Is there a healthy vision of mothering?' asks a woman over the other side of the room. Yes, says Polly Young-Eisendrath, but it's imperfect. It's difficult and relatively new. Mothers are giants in their children's psyches, and to withstand the rigours of mothering mothers need to know that they have a life, not simply to think that they need to get a life. For example, teenagers are pretty negative. (A ripple of assent runs through the room. Most of the women here are over forty.) Modern mothers 'cannot get feelings of competence from your experience of mothering, because the feedback takes so long coming'. For your own self-esteem it's good for the mother to have a role outside the home, when withstanding the onslaughts of a teenager. For example, says Polly Young-Eisendrath, when her teenagers say that they hate her she can say to them that they don't really hate her. That 'if I were the neighbour you would really like me'. There is more laughter.

Another woman says that at an archetype level it is very difficult to find positive images of mothering. And that it's harder at a collective level to find positive images of a good mother. Mother Earth, maybe, or the Virgin Mary – but where was the Virgin Mary's autonomy? Which brings you to the goddess images. 'At least some educated people are trying to take back goddess images,' says Polly Young-Eisendrath.

Polly Young-Eisendrath seems to believe that too much is demanded of mothers, and everyone else in the room seems to believe this as well. I believe it myself. But there appears to be no connection between the questions that are asked and the answers that are given. There is no plan; there are no handy hints on how to mother in the modern world. Yet everyone is riveted, and no one legs it during the coffee break. You can feel the longing in the room, not so much for a solution – these are parents and therapists after all – as for air-time.

What about the negative images of fathering, asks a man from the audience, citing Homer Simpson. Is the best that a modern father can hope for that he will be seen as a nice guy? Are we talking ourselves into a problem or are we in a problem? If we had really good child care in the workplace, says Polly Young-Eisendrath, it would substitute for the lack of community outside. Then children would be part of everyday concerns, the parents would worry less and the children would worry less. Separation anxiety is now part of the culture. Parents and children are always slightly anxious about where the other one is.

Later she talks about a woman who came to therapy because she had felt violent towards her child. Such feelings are inexpressible outside therapy, says Polly Young-Eisendrath, such is the idealized vision imposed on mothers. This woman was convinced that her son, Henry, was a genius who could learn Japanese. In fact Henry was an ordinary little boy who was out of control. In America Polly Young-

Eisendrath has observed the children of well-educated people behaving very badly in public. And even when they behave very badly, those children are indulged, because the parents feel guilty about leaving the child with minders if they are both working, and are convinced that discipline is cruel, whatever their childminding arrangements are. Henry's mother eventually went back to college, to do a master's degree in oriental languages, which had been her field of study before she had had Henry.

'So basically,' says a woman down the front with admirable clarity, 'you're saying that you're wrong if you stay at home and you're wrong if you go out to work.'

The very worst thing is for the mother to be isolated, says Polly Young-Eisendrath, who is like a piece of blond mercury.

A man asks about economic circumstances. Our 1937 constitution actually says that the mother should stay at home with the children. 'I have to be very careful here,' says the man, who rightly senses feminism all over the goddamn place. The women laugh. Until the 1970s female civil servants had to give up their jobs when they married, the man says. (Polly says that she had heard this last night.) The housing crisis here, says the man, has meant that women must go out to work. 'I don't think the individual has much to do with it,' he says. 'I think it it has more to do with economic planning.'

I get excited at this, because we might be on the edge of a discussion of how we're all being manipulated by market forces, and what a terrible con it all is. But no. Economics has always been the backdrop to the evolution of family and other relationships, says Polly Young-Eisendrath. It is part of her theory that full-time motherhood has only become idealized since the last world war, when women in America were sent back into the home to leave the job market open for returning male soldiers. Thanks a bunch, Polly.

During the coffee break I meet a woman in the canteen and she says that it isn't easy for fathers, either. Her son is a single father, and he wanted to be involved with his child, but the child's mother didn't want him to be. This woman had attended another lecture by Polly the previous evening. That talk was entitled 'Women and Desire: Beyond Wanting to Be Wanted.'

'There were so many OAPs there, I couldn't believe it,' says José. 'Of course we were offering a special price.' Pensioners were admitted to the talk last night for just £5, whereas the regular price was £12.

The woman I was talking to couldn't attend every one of Polly's lectures over the weekend. 'I have to go home some-time,' she said. Last night when she went to the lecture she had left a whole pile of ironing in the house; a pile full of things she'd been putting off ironing for ages. When she came in the door she found that her husband had done the lot.

Her daughter is a working wife, with a young child and another baby due in November. The woman, unlovely in a blue blazer and with close-cropped grey hair, had come today because she thought might pick up some things to give her daughter confidence, to make her feel better about being a working mother. Most of these young women now are doing everything, she said.

'They spend their lunch-hours thinking what they're going to get for the tea,' she said. Men don't spend their lunch-hours like that, I said. 'Although there are exceptions,' she said. Not many, I said, surprised by my own crankiness. 'I suppose I'm blessed,' she said.

Afterwards, there is a man waiting outside the front door in a small green car that is new. He's plump, in his sixties, dozing over a copy of the *Irish Times*. He looks like a nice man and he could be the husband of the devoted grandmother I had been speaking to earlier. Sure enough she gets into the shiny green car. He wakes up. They drive off together.

*

Every time I pick up the phone and stare into space for just six seconds I can hear my own voice saying my name. Then Conor Mullen tells me to please enter my password now. My six-digit password to my Eircom voice-mail is composed of the digits that make up my date of birth, which I cannot forget. But almost half the time Conor Mullen says: 'Sorry. That is not the correct password. Please. Re-enter. Your password now. If you have entered the wrong mailbox number, and would like to exit the system, please press star.' If you press the star key he says 'Goodbye', stonily.

'It *is* my correct password, you eejit,' I say. I have sworn at Conor Mullen from pay-phones and other people's offices all over the country. But the tape never changes. Sometimes Conor Mullen's voice says, 'You have. No. New messages in your mailbox.' Which is always a bit of a letdown.

Seán Hughes used to do a routine where he'd be sitting in his flat, on his own, and he'd pick up the phone to check that it was working, that he wasn't cut off from the exchange, just cut off from all his friends who hadn't bothered to ring. That was before voice-mail.

Sometimes the voice-mail voice says, 'The following message will be deleted from your mailbox. The message from. An unknown caller ...' and then I'm played the voice of a person whom I have forgotten, who left a message only seven days ago, but who is now unecessary, part of a crisis that has passed.

I had always imagined the owner of the voice-mail voice to be a grey-haired man in a drip-dry shirt – something like John Major's public image, pleasant but a bit dull and a little worried. Instead Conor Mullen is tall, blond and extremely handsome. He wears a leather jacket and, at the time I met him, was driving an old chocolate-brown Mercedes – 'The classic 200 fin-tail. It doesn't have leather seats or a walnut dash.' But now the Mercedes is getting tired and he thinks he'll get a Golf. 'Something with seatbelts in the back for the kids. For the first time I can afford to have a new car.'

Conor Mullen is now a household voice. 'I'd no idea that the Eircom voice-over would be so high profile. You become a hate figure,' he says. 'Taxi drivers say, "You're your man," which is fine. In the pub or whatever, people say "I was only talking to you today," but people can be quite rude sometimes and say things like "We're fucking sick listening to you."'

'I would have thought that the voice sounds quite different to my own but I was on the B&I ferry once, just hanging out on deck, and this guy came up to me and said, "You sound just like Conor Mullen." He was a voice-over head.

'I do sort of Irish neutral. I don't do a lot of character stuff, I do mostly straight stuff. I do a lot of young corporate stuff. Banks, cars. I do a lot of end lines. You know the line at the end of the ad which tells you to stay at Jury's Hotel? I do a lot of them. I used to do the *Irish Times*. I still do, if Owen Roe is away filming. "For the Times We Live In",' he says suddenly, and helpfully.

It sounds peculiar said live like this, in a pub at lunchtime. It makes you feel that the *Irish Times* is more fragile than you had previously thought.

'Mazda: That Certain Feeling,' he says. 'Let's Talk Phones.' I feel stupid writing this down.

'I do Breo, "Refreshment through Colour". And Nivea, "For Men Who Dare to Care".' He laughs as he says the Nivea one. 'You know the AIB ad. "Are You Ready For The Big Drop?"'

It's about pensions. Guaranteed to give you a shiver just when you think things are going well.

'Well, I'm the stupid one in that, the one who goes, "What Big Drop?"' I do young, smooth, warm. It's all right to go and buy this product. Do not be afraid. There's nothing wrong with that. The National Car Test ad with the Madness music. Benylin. I seem to do a lot of cold and flu remedies.'

I think of my boyfriend going in to the chemist's and asking for something for a dry, tickly cough, and the girls behind the counter laughing at him, and him saying, 'Yeah, just like the ad.' The market in male hypochondria is a rich one.

'I do the VHI: "It's Nice to Know VHI Is There." I do Vienetta ice cream. Really, it's reliable, maybe young with a few quid.'

Like you, I say.

'It's just the crumbs,' he says.

I saw Conor Mullen before he became the ex-husband in *Badger*, on another British television series called *Reckless*, a romantic drama which I watched closely. He didn't look so handsome in *Reckless* – he must be the opposite of photogenic. He smokes Camel cigarettes and so do I while we are talking, bumming them off him. His voice is both lower and louder than it is on the voice-mail system. In the flesh it's got a lot of reverb. Just as models and television presenters talk about their own hair and face as 'the hair, the face', so Conor Mullen refers to his voice as 'the voice'. Throughout our meeting I waver between drooling schoolgirl and brisk matron, touching all points of female flutter in between.

Conor Mullen also played the company sergeant-major, Alan Fitzpatrick, in the series *Soldier, Soldier*. I would have thought that he he was a bit young to be a sergeant-major. He thought so too. They gave the sergeant-major a sixteen-year-old son in the series, which he thought was a bit much. But soldiers join up when they're eighteen. They marry at twenty. They become adults young. Not like us.

Conor Mullen grew up in Sutton, a middle-class suburb in north-east Dublin. 'I got into acting because I had been working with my dad and it didn't work out. It was the Seventies and everything was shit. Everybody was depressed. It was always raining. You were always sitting in Bewley's, soaking wet, smoking. My mate and I heard about acting classes and we thought we'd give it a shot. It was something to do.'

He went to America. 'By the time I came back I was able to get a part in *Macbeth*' – he doesn't say 'The Scottish Play', as old-style superstitious actors do. 'No, I wasn't part of the Abbey company. There were only four or maybe six actors left in the company at the stage. We were mostly freelance.'

His career in Britain – 'I commute a lot' – took off as a direct result of his involvement in voice-over work. 'In your twenties you're the young juve. You can play the son, you can play the boyfriend. When I hit my thirties it all started, you know, it all started going a bit quiet. I started doing voice-overs. Actors had a kind of snobbery about voice-overs then. It was, "We don't do voice-overs". It was kind of like selling out. But actors became more professional, and it opened up, from four guys doing everything to more actors doing it to supplement their income.

'But I made a deal with myself that I wouldn't turn down an

acting job in favour of voice-overs, and in the end my career in England opened up precisely because I could afford to take the work I wanted to. Voice-overs can take actors off the breadline.'

Voice-over work helped Conor Mullen in this way. The money he earned from voice-overs allowed him to take a job in play by a young playwright with no money, whose name was Conor McPherson. Conor Mullen went straight to the Bush Theatre in London, where there were casting directors in every night. 'We all got loads of telly out of it.'

He agrees that since he started in the voice-over business advertisements have probably become straighter. There are fewer funny ads, fewer distinctive accents unless they're being used by idiot characters who are shortly to see the light when they are informed about the product being advertised. Older voice-over actors are convinced of this, and that the advertising agencies have been beaten into submission. Everyone agrees that the client has become much more involved. In the old days clients wouldn't come to a recording session, or if they did, would sit quietly in the corner. Now, 'when I'm recording I can have three or four people directing me', says Conor Mullen.

When he heard that Telecom needed a new voice, he submitted a demo tape which included the statement 'The number you have dialled has been changed.' That's how he got the job.

'I think the voice has to be within a certain range of pitch. If the tone of my voice goes in to that band, they choose me.'

Paul Ellis, who works for McConnells advertising agency, which has the Eircom account, says that this isn't actually true: 'The vast majority of voices fit into that range. Mullen was chosen for having one of the most accessible, friendly voices around at the moment. You can listen to it day in and day out without getting annoyed. It was its non-irritant value above everything else. The clients chose the voice from our recommendations. It was a one hundred per cent emotional, cultural, rather than technical decision.'

*

In September 1999 Dr Marie Laffoy of the Eastern Helath Board asked the board to advise parents against placing children on sunbeds prior to making their first holy communions and confirmations. Dr Laffoy had heard about this from three sources. Firstly, a dermatologist in Hume Street hospital. Secondly, her own daughter, then making her confirmation in Dundrum, who came home and said that everyone in her class was getting sunbeds in preparation for the event, and why couldn't she? (Dr Laffoy says you have to allow for children's exaggeration on this one, but even so.) Thirdly, the head of the Irish Association of Cosmetic Practitioners rang Dr Laffoy at work. Dr Laffoy says that she was afraid that the woman was going to shout at her for ruining the sunbed business, but on the contrary, the woman was ringing to encourage her, because, she said, too many unscrupulous sunbed traders were putting children on them and it was a disgrace. Could Dr Laffoy please issue some guidelines which advise against artificial tanning for the under-eighteens?

*

Brian Rigby sells Spirit door to door. Spirit is a cut-price phone service piggy-backing on Eircom lines. You get cheaper rates on international calls, calls to mobiles, and on what used to be known as trunk calls down the country. You dial the 13011 prefix before making those calls. Brian says that for local calls Eircom is still cheapest.

Brian Rigby is small and slightly round – 'my weight is a constant problem'. He has the reassuring accent of the English Midlands, the Birmingham accent that seems to have been created for telling the truth; the sort of accent we hear in soap operas all the time, the way an adored soccer defender might talk. Therefore being an Englishman in Ireland has never been a problem for Brian on the doorsteps. Brian has other problems on the doorsteps. 'The Irish don't like being sold to,' he says. 'You have to be a bit blasé, and let them close the sale themselves. You have to wait until they say, "What do I have to do to join up?"'

When I meet him Brian is living in Newbridge, County Kildare, about thirty miles from Dublin. He's sharing a house with his friend Rory, the man who brought him to Ireland. But Brian plans to move to Dublin. He thinks that Newbridge is a little bit small. He's recently broken up with a Newbridge girl. Brian thinks that Irish girls are a little bit conservative.

'That's my car over there,' he said as we walked down the street in a deluge of rain. It's a red Peugeot. 'I never buy new cars. Ten thousand pounds! You could travel the world for ten thousand pounds.' He has a fringe, large eyes and a direct gaze. The edges of his top front teeth slope in towards each other at an angle, and look sharp.

Brian will tell you about his sales technique. He's a tireless talker, virtually unstoppable. He's an area manager with a team of ten young, self-employed agents under him. 'I'm the only area manager who won't take people over forty. When I'm forty-five I want to be much more financially secure. If you're door-knocking in your fifties maybe you haven't made the most of your opportunities. Young people are smiley. Young people create a better atmosphere. I've seen some older door-knockers who are not very good. If I was working a country area I would have people over forty. In the city your introduction is shorter and you have less time to impress.

'To get on my team they must have a mobile phone. I need them to have some sales experience or to have a goal – like travelling for example.

'There is a high turnover. They go because their heads go. Sometimes they just need a holiday. I say, "Just remember when you come back it's going to be tough." I want them working five hours a day, five days a week. That's a standard minimum. Otherwise your're not doing yourself justice, you're not doing the job justice.'

He's had to explain his methods many, many times. He draws a flow chart into my notebook.

In the first box he writes INTRO. 'This is the most important part. Get this right and the product sells itself. It has to be bright, it has to be positive, it has to be upbeat. I tell them who I am and what I'm going to do. If you're invited in, then nine times out of ten you'll sell.

'Then you move on to SALES PITCH, PART I. That's how it works. Installation is free. No change of phone equipment or of phone number. Try us. We're lots cheaper.

'Then you QUALIFY. You establish their call pattern. Do they have a sister in America? Do they call the UK a lot? Sometimes qualifying can take four times as long as the intro and the sales pitch part one.

'Then you move on to SALES PITCH, PART II. You include the price here.

'Then you CLOSE, deal with any OBJECTIONS. Ask about NEXT DOOR.

'Then you do the RE-HASH. Have they any problems? You tell them they'll get a call tomorrow, to join them up to the system. They will be feeling a bit guilty now, for signing up. "Oh I forgot to ask this ..." Or, "My husband's coming home in an hour." Sometimes they ring up and cancel.

'This work's more than telephone sales. It's by by far the most successful form of selling in the domestic market. Basically the technique is to invade your space and sell.

'If someone's rude I don't make another call immediately. I go and sit in the car for twenty minutes. For the first five minutes I'm angry. For the second five minutes I say, "What am I doing this for? What am I doing door-knocking for?"

'For the third five minutes I'm in a trance, like this' – he stares fixedly over my right shoulder. It's a bit disquieting. 'For the fourth five minutes I'm thinking positive. I don't put a foot out of the car until I've done that. For door-knocking you must have your composure.

'You can never be rude to someone, if they're rude to you. It's what we cope with all the time. How you cope with it is you take the mickey amongst yourselves. It's like a fireman who goes to an accident where someone has lost an arm, and he makes jokes about him being harmless. It's the same in door-knocking.

'Body language is another thing – ours, not theirs. I was out with one of our team the other day, and she's on the doorstep like this' – he folds his arms. 'I had to nudge her and say, "Get your arms down, be open." Eye contact is another one. Look at them and nod. If they're looking away you're losing them.

Sometimes Brian almost despairs of the general public. 'If they were prepared to give you the time you could save them money. It's like the old saying, most people are too busy making a living to make any money. I've done the jobs where you're earning £200 a week – they're not worth doing. Too busy and too tired to make money. It's a kind of attitude of life, and I can relate to that. They're working ten hours a day and they're stressed out to the max. The last thing you want to do at the end of the day is to talk to someone about your phone bill or something like that. That reluctance also comes from the culture, and the fact that we're selling a new service.'

He never despairs of his sales team, though.

'My main problem with my team is getting them out of bed in the morning. Because they are a young team they stay up late. I have to work very hard in motivating them. We have two area management meetings a week. I set them goals.

'If at the end of the week someone doesn't do so good you have the support of people round you. There's a marvellous atmosphere, it's not "Oh, look you're not very good." The agenda weekly meeting is in a pub. I say, "That's a good effort," and I'll chat with you there. Or you're struggling with your pitch. I'll put you with Roger, he's got a good pitch. I'd never get rid of someone for their technique, but for their attitude.'

Brian is very clear as to where his organizational abilities come from. 'As a young fellow of eighteen, nineteen, twenty I did a lot of competition fishing. I got to a very high level. I thought I could have made it to international level, although maybe that's unrealistic. In fishing you've got to be organized, you've got to professional. You might cast over under that big tree, see if they're are any fish hiding in the water under there. It's trial and error. It's the same with marketing and sales. Try it. It doesn't work, try something else. I was thinking "How can I catch more fish?" all the time. That's my nature. I met people who could teach me how.'

Brian's very organized, but he's also very tense. 'I suffer from stress. The Irish have a more relaxed way of doing things. They say, "Later, so what?" To de-stress I go fishing. I'm a member of a gym. Exercising is very, very, very helpful. I go three times a week. I eat like a madman and I drink like a madman, but at least with going to the gym I feel I've got the weight under control.

'My goal is to buy a property back home, in Birmingham, within the next ten years, on a 50 per cent mortgage. I shall rent it out. My goal is to be happy. I'm not career-minded. If I were to take ten grand you could live a good life for ten years on that in Thailand. Just chill out at times. If you think carefully you can work for one year and live well for ten.'

Although he doesn't say so, Brian's entrance into the telecom business mirrors that of David Ryan, Spirit's chief executive in Ireland. Spirit is a brand of Interoute Ireland, which received the first general telecommunications licence after deregulation on 1 December 1998.

David Ryan is thirty-seven. It was he who came up with the name Spirit for the Irish branch of Interoute International. 'He was actually meditating when it came to him,' says Jill down the phone. 'I don't know what type of meditation he does. It's alternative.'

David Ryan left Dublin when he was eighteen and went to Australia. The Australian phone market was deregulated in 1991. David Ryan worked for Telstra, which had previously had the monopoly in Australia, and Optimis, their new rival in the phone market. He also worked for SingTel in Singapore. 'He worked in a lot of the de-regulating markets in south-east Asia,' says Jill, who has a young Dublin voice with a dying fall. 'He took the model of direct sales from Australia.' And he took Brian Rigby as well.

'I got into door-knocking because I was backpacking round Austalia,' says Brian Rigby. 'In England I sold insurance for a few years. I sold block paving products between working as a waiter. In Australia I picked apples in a place called Batlow. Picking apples is work that keeps you fit.'

In Australia, just like David Ryan, their future boss, Brian and his friend Rory worked for Telstra and then for Optimis.

Brian Rigby looks more square sitting down. He uses his hands when he talks. He draws diagrams, he illustrates his points by moving things around the table of the café where we are sitting. In the café people are slumped in their chairs, reading, smoking, relaxing; Brian Rigby is concentrating. He is very good at explaining.

Brian left Austalia because 'the commissions wasn't that quite right. With Optimis you'd get $27 per churn [i.e. per phone number brought into the company system]. My best was eleven a day with Optimis and my best with Telstra was eighteen. Telstra paid $12 to $14 per churn. Australians are tough on the outside but not on the inside. You could bully them.'

I ask for an example of this. Brian Rigby sits up straighter in his seat, and his voice becomes louder. He holds out a piece of paper with a stern look. 'Can you see the money you'd be saving there? And can you see the money you'd be saving there? Why aren't you prepared to change? Is there something I haven't explained? Are you ready to start filling out the form? Oh, oh,' Brian cries, acting out the part of the apologetic customer. He scribbles with an imaginary pen. I am frightened out of my wits.

'Rory was manager of pre-paid card division in Spirit in Dublin. He gave me the call, I flew over for the interview and I liked it, I liked what I saw. What did I see? I saw lots and lots of young people, for one thing. I started work as an area manager and I'm happy in that role.'

He gives me the re-hash now, a little early: 'The Spirit residential phone service, at the moment, we're the largest company because we took the direct-sales route. We knock on your door and the next thing you know you've Spirit. David Ryan, he came up with the name Spirit. He's one of the best talkers I've seen. He genuinely wanted to build a different kind of telecom company. It's all sales talk at the end of the day, but you can believe it as well.

'I don't believe the Irish phone market will become as fractured as the American one. The Irish won't let that happen, they're so much harder to sell to, they wouldn't let it snowball. Can you remember your old telephone bill? Phoning Antarctica, the US, Joe Bloggs down the road, and it all jumbled in together? It was a pathetic piece of bill. Even now that bill isn't set out particularly well, but it is an improvement.

'Interoute has the largest fibre-optic cable in Europe. To see the way telecommunications is going to go you'd have to watch *Star Trek* to imagine. It's all copper cables now, and Ireland's going to have to upgrade. Look.' He puts a biro on the table between us. 'Copper cable is a thin country lane.' He puts a sheet of paper next to the biro. 'Fibre-optic is a motorway, it's that much wider. It'll be able to carry voice data and everything.'

So much future, it'd wear you out. Brian Rigby thinks he'll be in the telecommunications business for quite some time.

'I'm from a place called Aldrich-by-Walsall, near Birmingham. It's quite a big place, a lot of rural area around it when I was growing up. It's probably the size of Newbridge. I'm thirty-three. I would have been ten or nine when my parents got the phone put in. I remember we had incoming calls only for a while. My parents didn't particularly use the phone, but I did, particularly when I started to get involved in competition fishing. I remember my mate Paul Shore's phone number was 55301, and I probably made my first phone call to him. They got their phone slightly before ours. I seem to remember ringing Paul Shore up and saying, "This is good, isn't it, the telephone?"'

*

'This is Gordon Mathews. Thank you for calling. Please leave your name and number at the tone, and I'll get back to you. If your message is urgent press the U key, that is the 8 key on your phone, and, through the miracle of electronics, my cell phone will go off and I'll hear your message and get back to you even quicker. Have a great day.'

Gordon Mathews, an engineer from Texas, invented voice-mail while he was working for 3M. I left four messages, two marked as urgent by the 8 key on my telephone. But he never called. He sent e-mails. His e-mail address is vmfather@ aol.com

*

You'd know Anna and Eva are foreigners. They're not just punctual, they are early for our meeting. They're tiny, dressed in layers of grey. Their pelvises are so narrow that you find yourself wondering if they're wearing children's jeans. Anna and Eva have the seriousness of foreigners, too. No make-up, good skin, disciplined hair. I order three biscuits in the pub where we are sitting, and wolf mine down. I end up taking home the other two biscuits in the pocket of my walking jacket, which suddenly seems huge and tent-like. My coffee is gulped in seconds. Perhaps this is is what people mean when they say Ireland has an oral tradition. Anna and Eva don't have it at all. Anna and Eva sit over their lemonades, and leave them largely untouched after an hour.

Anna is Spanish, Eva is Italian. They work in an interna-tional call centre situated just outside Dublin. For each European language they speak their employers add another £1,000 to their salary. 'We sit in two big rooms, divided into markets. Six in a group, three facing three. There are flags hanging everywhere, to encourage you.'

In the early days of January 1993, when Anna and Eva were still at school in Andalucia and Rome respectively, two senior managers addressed the board of the IDA (Industrial Development Authority), which was holding its annual meeting in the Grand Hotel in Malahide, outside Dublin. A bleak place in January. The two senior managers had been given a year out to research emerging structures in the American market.

They came home and told the IDA that, whether they liked it or not, the future lay in what were then known as call centres. In multi-lingual, pan-European call centres, to be exact. The IDA then set out to target some of the Fortune 500 companies. By the end of 1993 it had drawn up a hit list of the companies they thought likely to move within Europe.

The IDA began cold-calling these companies, saying: 'Why don't you centralize your European operations in Ireland?' The IDA had costed the concept of making such a move for each company. In most cases it was able to tell the company that it would save 30 to 40 per cent of its overall costs of dealing with customers in Europe by centralizing in Ireland. The easiest targets in the IDA push were the reservation centres. The reservation centres had been thinking about making such a move. But, as Colm Donlon of the IDA puts it, 'they had lots of fears'. Colm Donlon has a fearless, relaxed voice. He sounds as if he has his feet up on the desk. He's the IDA's press offi-cer. Even I have heard of him.

'There's something you should know,' says Eva. 'We can't control the pace of the calls coming through.'

'Beep, there is a call,' says Anna

'You can press the personal button and go to the toilet,' says Eva.

'The beep gets into your brain,' says Anna

'I used to dream of the mask, the head-set. I went on holi-days and I saw it all the time. Yes, it is a mask. In Italian you say *maschera*,' says Eva.

'You can see the calls waiting. We have a big screen on the wall,' says Anna.

'I've seen thirty calls there,' says Eva.

'I've seen twenty and it was a really big problem,' says Anna.

'At peak hours there could be forty or fifty calls for each country,' says Eva.

Anna and Eva earn a maximum of £275 per week, includ-ing bonuses, for working a seven-and-a-half-hour day. They don't get paid for their lunch hour, and a ten-minute break every two and a half hours doesn't leave them enough time to get to the smoking area. Their shifts are unpredictable. 'It took a month for me once to be able to book a holiday,' says Anna. 'They wouldn't tell me what the shifts were going to be, I couldn't book my holiday tickets. That's very bad manage-ment.'

'The idea was to set up flagship names,' says Colm Donlon. 'Like UPS [United Parcel Service], they were one of the early movers. Hertz were prestigious. American Airlines was very important. Japanese Airlines and others followed.'

'There are six hundred or seven hundred people working there,' says Eva. She and Anna look at each other gravely, checking to see which is the right number. They do this often, like solemn twins.

'If you want to get a bonus you've got to deal with eighty calls a day,' says Anna. 'You've got to sell, sell, sell. All the team leaders are women. All the senior managers are men. Even the HR manager is a man, which is unusual.' HR stands for human resources, which is the new term for personnel.

In the past five years, as Colm Donlon puts it, Ireland has 'wiped the market' in European call centres. The main competition came from Holland. In order to take on the Dutch the IDA had to get Telecom Éireann, as it then was, to provide a special package for prospective call centres. A package that would would provide volume pricing and special service. This they did.

In Anna and Eva's call centre the calls are monitored, which Eva thinks would be illegal in Italy. 'They monitor about four calls a month. They hide when they're monitoring you. They go to another market and they sit down at those desks, and they have a password to get into your call.'

'My team leader monitored me and I knew,' says Anna. 'I knew she was monitoring someone because I could see her and she was not talking, she was just writing down things. She was a friend of mine. Afterwards she said, 'Aha, I was monitoring you,' and so that was all right. But it can be embarrassing.'

'They go through a check-list and if it's not right, forget it, you don't get your bonus,' says Eva.

'And you can forget some of the questions on the check-list,' says Anna. 'They say we should soft-sell, encourage the customer to buy more from us, which I don't like. I don't think it's good.'

'Our team leaders are very, very disorganized,' says Eva.

'You get some things changed from one day to another,' says Anna. 'I think that's bullying, as well. You can't do anything about it. If you're taking seventy calls a day you find it hard to keep up.'

They acknowldege that the workers are also disorganized. In America, call centres are frequently staffed by old-age pensioners and part-time female workers who are supposedly not relying on the work for a living wage. Anna and Eva agree that unions are strong in both Italy and Spain. But call centres in Ireland are difficult to unionize because 'we are foreigners, moving all the time. To us it's an alternative to waitressing. If there are problems with the company we elect one person to go to the management, but then maybe it's not good for that person.'

Many of the foreign workers, with two European languages, are offered incentive and settlement packages to come and work in Ireland. And many of them hop from one call centre to another, gathering incentive payments, and leaving the call centres with a recruitment nightmare.

'Our proposal was based on the American companies accepting that Europe was now a single market,' says Colm Donlon. 'Often the companies were keeping offices in European countries open simply to placate politicians in that country.' A foreign concept.

'The Spanish and Italian customers want the service to be round the corner,' says Eva. 'They can't understand that you're not in the same country they are in. So then you tell them, "I'm not in the same country. I'm in Ireland." They're so surprised.'

'The companies must be making a lot of money,' says Anna, 'since they centralized all the offices into one place, here. But the customer is not different.'

'In Italy there were fourteen or fifteen people in the Milan office,' says Eva. 'They knew the customer. We don't know anybody. The customers treat me really well, which creates some problems because if you get more customers, you get more sales calls.'

I had heard that Xerox's call-centre staff are being trained in by the staff who were being made redundant in offices round Europe, leading to what one recruitment consultant called 'a bad atmosphere. You can imagine what it's like for the people who are losing their jobs. They're aggressive and disappointed.' Xerox strenuously denies this.

'There are four official languages in Spain,' says Anna. 'Most of our customers are Catalan, for some reason, but our team leaders wanted us to speak Spanish, you know, Castillian, to all of them. There was no resolution and the customers were very unhappy. So when I heard Catalan accents or Catalan names I would speak Catalan to them as best I could. They were very happy, and when they heard that we were in Ireland they were also very happy. But officially nothing has been done.'

'The normal lifespan of a call-centre worker is about six months, but after about two weeks you want to go,' says Eva. 'If you are somebody with a degree you will die there.' Eva has a continental European's belief in intellectual development. 'Repeating the same thing eighty times a day drives you crazy. And you are restricted physically, you can't even go to the toilet when you want.

'They warned me that it was routine work; I thought it would be like clerical work, I wasn't prepared for it. I had the feeling I was in a factory. When I finish the Italian phone calls there's ten English phone calls, say one of them is from Wales. They think they're calling a centre in England, they don't want to talk to a foreigner. Some people just put down the phone.'

'Physically it's not as bad as restaurant work,' says Anna. 'It's stressful because it's boring, it's routine. Nine months ago our managers started to try and vary the work. They're not stupid. I think they are getting desperate. They realized that it was like an assembly line, and it is. That's why so many people are leaving. That's why there are so many people phoning in sick. Absenteeism is the word, exactly.'

The IDA didn't want to stop at call centres, although it acknowledges there have been some problems with training and conditions within them. The IDA has moved on to shared service centres, clearing-houses for a company's backroom administrative work. Citibank, says Colm Donlon, is the best example of this.

The next step in the IDA's development strategy is the promotion of e-commerce centres. The Global Crossing fibre-optic cable is already installed in Eircom's headquarters at City West. The lines between call centres, shared service centres and e-commerce centres have been blurring for a while now, and the sectors are beginning to merge. 'By the year 2005 if you are able to distinguish between those different sectors then we are no good as a country,' says Colm Donlon. I put down the phone to him feeling strangley depressed.

Anna and Eva are sensible rather than cheerful. In Spain, Anna says, call centres are 'coming up like mushrooms'. They walk off together, tiny figures. They both carry mobile phones.

*

The first thing that strikes you when you walk into the nursing home is that there are no voices. The phone only rings once in the entire time you are there. The television is playing Irish music, and a couple of old people sit around silently in chairs.

They are very pale. My friend's voice is strong in here. 'Hi Dad. What happened his hands?'

'What happened his hands? What happened his hands?' echoes the staff member who let us in. She doesn't answer the question, though. My friend's father's hands are covered in dark purple bruises. Maybe he had to be restrained, says my friend later. He can get aggressive and he's a big guy. Maybe they're injection marks, I say later. There are an awful lot of them.

Lily's is the only loud voice here but Lily is slightly deaf and deaf people often talk loudly – they can't modulate their voices. 'This is a very sad place,' shouts Lily, as we sit in the middle of the hall. 'I say to the woman who owns it, "You should be here more." She's never here, and you've got to be here.' Lily loves my friend's father. 'I love him like a sister,' she says. Lily is ninety-seven, older than everybody else. She doesn't know how to use the phone here, she says. Her sister-in-law phones every day. When I ask about phoning Lily a nurse tells me that there are telephones in all the rooms. But when I phone later in the evening with an address Lily had asked for, they have to wheel her to the main phone, in the hall. And then Lily can't hear me. 'I can't hear him,' she says. 'Who is he?'

I move a chair for a woman with a walking frame. 'Thank you,' she says. 'Will you put me to bed?' It is a child's voice. I say I'll get a nurse. Lily says there are no nurses, but I run to get one. In here, if you're under sixty and mobile then everyone thinks you are a nurse. In a separate development I get a glass from the deserted kitchen for an old man who is sitting in the television room amongst people with their heads bowed. (Lily says they always look as if they're at Mass, whether they're at Mass or not.) The old man says he was rather hoping that I'd pour the mineral water as well. I do.

'I can't go to the toilet,' says Lily in what is a good imitation of a whisper. 'Because of my leg. But no one takes you. You're waiting all day.'

Lily is one of the few people here who is not demented. She says she is up at seven in the morning and can be left for up to an hour, 'excuse me, on the commode'. They don't wash Lily, they just, she says, wipe her at the back. She says her clothes have been stolen. She says this is a sad place. She says Mass is so quiet. One time the priest announced her death at Mass. She told him that he needed a rest. The priest said to Lily that he knew that he needed a rest, but the bishop had sent him here to say Mass. Lily says Mass is so silent, she'd like some young people in singing 'Hail Glorious Saint Patrick.' Lily's rosary beads are draped across her handbag. On the back of her handbag, written in biro, is the name and address of the most prestigious person Lily knows.

'Now, Peggy,' says the woman I had called – and how do I know if she's a nurse or not? She is going into the room of the woman who had asked me to put her to bed. She's talking too loudly. I don't like it. 'You want me to put you to BED,' she says. The door is half open. There is no privacy here. Privacy is gone.

They're not well, they're not well, says Lily. They walk into her room in the middle of the night. It can be startling. The roof in her room is leaking rainwater on to her bed. Lily speaks French and German. The woman who asked me to put her to bed also speaks German. 'Arthur told me he is coming to Vienna,' says the lady who asked me to put her to bed. 'Do you think they'll let him come in?'

Oh yes, say myself and Lily, Arthur will definitely get in. 'Arthur is great,' says the lady. 'But don't tell him that, he'll only get conceited and he's conceited enough already.'

Once Lily fell off the train to Bray; that was when the trouble with her leg may have started. She fell into a snow drift in Switzerland and had to shout 'Au secours, au secours' to passing skiers. She set her hair on fire once when she was curling it in papers too close to the fire. She had to have an Eton crop. 'These are the things that happen to me,' she says.

My friend's father, who is a tall man, walks into a wrought-iron bracket lamp which is placed high on the wall, and says nothing. My friend removes the lamp from the wall. We leave for a drive.

When we come back Lily is gone and the smell of urine is palpable. As I wait for my friend to come out of her father's room another woman on a walking frame comes out of her room. She is wearing a jumper and knickers and her legs are very thin. 'Nurse, nurse,' she is crying like a child. These are the things that happen to me. I run to get another member of staff, who is eastern European. 'Sure they were all Filipino a couple of weeks ago,' says my friend later. They talk in the woman's room with the door open. 'It's at the laundry,' says the eastern European girl. 'Cover me up, cover me up,' cries the woman. Another member of staff sweeps past me into the room and closes the door.